One Day in the Life of Ivan Dentistovich and Other Related *and NOT* Stories ©

An atypical collection of short stories

D1568781

Jonathan L. Macarus

Larry & Jackie,
Thank you for all of your prayers
& support, and the encouragement of
your faith. All the best, and
TRAVEL MERCIES Too!

:-)

Jon

To all of my friends and family who did more than just put up with me over these many years, but also aided me in providing material and in the formation of who I am today. *(You see, I am not the only one to blame.)* I would like to add a special thanks: to Matt Robertson for his guidance in formatting; to my mom and Kathy Jacomet for their help in editing this "piece of work;" to my wife, Mary, who forgave me for her not understanding the fine print on "Let me Take You Away from All of This!" when it turned out that the actual *"going to"* place was Russia; and to God, for without him, none of this would have been possible. *(Take it up with Him.)*

This book is dedicated to my wonderful father. I will miss you dearly. To all those who attended, wrote and spoke recently at his memorial; thanks. Your presence and sharing meant a great deal to us, and we were deeply moved. To be so beautifully sent off, is not only an honor, but also something to live for.

One Day in the Life of Ivan Dentistovich and Other Related *and NOT* Stories

An atypical collection of short stories

My Brother and the Great Pillow Fight.................................5

My First Trip to the Dentist . . . in Russia...........................11

On Teeth and Heroes..17

One Day in the Life of Ivan Dentistovich...........................20

In Defense of the Fatherland?!?..25

Hemorrhoids and Heartaches...29

I Can't Believe It. My Mother was Right...........................36

My Conclusions..45

My Sister the Clown Maker...52

The Case of the Significant Error..57

Travel Mercies...61

How to Sell a Car in Russia...76

The Technical Inspection...104

My Brother and the Great Pillow Fight

My Brother:

My brother, Jordan, is two and a half years older than I. Unfortunately that will always be the case. Now that we are both much older, that difference seems very small. Yet when we were young, it made all the difference in the world.

Back then, growing up as the younger brother had its disadvantages, too. I was smaller, slower, and not as strong as my brother *(or my sisters for that matter)*. And, as if that were not enough, my brother just happened to be one of the fastest kids in school and in the neighborhood. He had lightning reflexes. So, as you might expect, I found myself often fighting a losing battle whenever it came to *any* fight between us, including those with pillows.

The Pillow Fights:

As we grew, these disadvantages continued to be a source of humiliation. Time after time, upon entering into battle, all pillows being equal, my brother was able to inflict two or three times the number of blows, and with more force, than I was ever able to muster. What this meant was that I would be left staggering and rearing on a good day and crumpled on the floor with the pillow over my head on the bad ones.

So, for many years, my honor went miserably defended. Until having been beaten enough, I had sense beaten into me *(perhaps the old adage came true)*. I finally reasoned that to do battle with my brother with conventional pillow weaponry was a hopeless cause. I had to think of something to increase my advantage. *(Perhaps this had a big part to play in my later becoming a scientist interested in advanced technology. Only God really knows.)* I started to think how I could use advanced technology to increase the force and impact of my ordinary pillow. After some time, I really do not remember how long, it finally came to me. And I believe a smile spread across my face, much like the smile on a particular creature's face when he had finally decided what to do in order to stop Christmas from coming . . . .

I was going nuclear.

The idea seemed ingenious. I would get one of my mom and dad's larger pillows and then stuff it with clothes, including a pair of my old blue jeans, to make it about four times as heavy as my brother's pillow. Now, of course, not fully understanding all of the physics behind momentum *(that of mass times velocity)*, the basics were clear enough to a boy my age: the bigger and heavier the pillow, the more my brother would feel it. Yet, I still needed an extra advantage. I had to strike without warning or provocation. I had to strike preemptively . . . .

D-Day, The Great Pillow Fight:

I was so anxious and eager to test out my new weapon

that it was with difficulty that I hid my smile and excitement that morning. I could feel my heart racing, knowing that today, after school, World War III was going to take place. That day, I ran home in order to beat my brother to the house. I could hardly wait as I stood in my room with the door slightly cracked to listen for my brother's return. I was even so anxious, I could hear my heart beating hard; and I was trying so hard not to breathe too loudly. Time seemed to slow down as the ringing in my ears grew louder. I heard the front door open, and my heart jumped. I grabbed my loaded-down pillow and stood with my hand on the doorknob waiting for the right moment.

My brother eventually climbed the stairs, went into his bedroom and closed the door. Now was my chance. I opened my door slowly and quietly and then snuck *(or sneaked if you prefer; as a child, I did a lot of sneaking and, at the time, did not concern myself with the proper grammar or spelling of the situation)* down the hall towards his room. I grabbed his doorknob and set the pillow over my shoulder in battle readiness. I turned the knob slowly and braced myself for what was about to take place. I took a deep breath, crashed through the door, and shouted at the same time. For a moment, time stood still as I stood there with the pillow over my shoulder and my back straight as if a superhero bursting through a metal door and standing there majestic and mighty with his cape flowing in the wind. Time also stood still for my brother, as confusion turned into comprehension in his eyes. Then, with time moving slowly forward, he started for his pillow. He was quick, but not quick enough for the moments in time gained by my surprise. I swung and struck first sending him careening off his intended path with more force than he ever expected. Stun and surprise were written all over his face—victory and joy over mine . . . .

Unfortunately, however, my joy was short lived. My understanding of basic physics was about to be tested and found wanting, as I was forced to discover that I needed to know more about momentum and inertia than I did. In particular, with inertia, that a body in motion wants to stay in motion and a body at rest likes it that way. In other words, I miscalculated and failed to take into account the extra effort and time it would require to wield and put in motion such a highly advanced, heavy pillow. And thus in rearming my pillow to its attacking position behind my shoulder, my brother had time to reach his own.

He made a move to swing and our blows struck simultaneously: his to my head and face, and mine to his shoulder and side. His blow caused only a minor stun, whereas mine sent him staggering again to one side. Things weren't looking all that bad at this time. However, my brother recovered quickly, and before I had a chance to ready my pillow for its next strike, he delivered another blow to the head. This had the unfortunate effect of further slowing the readying of my own pillow. By the time I was ready to swing again, my brother had struck perhaps one or two times more with his lightning quickness and strength. I swung, but this time my movements were slower, and my brother only took a glancing blow. He then delivered about five blows to my one. The situation was beginning to look grim. Now with my highly advanced, technological pillow, I was down to one blow to my brothers five. On top of that, my strength was waning from the extra weight of the pillow and my brother's blows. After one more melee round, it was all over. Once again, I was winded and down on the floor in a heap, hoping that my brother would have mercy and accept a truce. So much for technology; it was back to the drawing board and my room with my humility and shame. Who cares about honor anyway?

A Few Conclusions:

I wonder if we, as a nation, shouldn't take this important military lesson to heart. It seems we may spend so much time and energy on new, advanced technology in planes and weaponry that are, in the end, more likely to break and are, by nature, harder and more difficult to maintain in battle.

Perhaps instead, we would do better to stick with the conventional technology that we know and can throw at the enemy in good number and can keep more in the air at any given time. But I digress slightly; and I am not sure that full analogies can be made between sibling rivalry, pillow fights, and national strategies. For what I chose to do next, in my battle with my brother, may not always be an available option for a nation . . . .

A Final Strategy:

Having endured the loss again at my brother's feet and discouraged by the failure of technology, I was in need of an alternative solution. I chose to go back to the regular, conventional pillow for its ease of transport, delivery, and stealth. How I was to use it would be the trick.

Much like the previous attack, I crept up to his room

unheard. I swung open his door and leveled two blows from my pillow before my brother had time to reach his. I then stopped my attack, turned and ran, closing his door behind me and at the same time shouting "Mom!!!!" and making for my room as fast as I could, slamming and locking the door behind me. Of course, the tone in which I shouted made it appear to my mother, who was downstairs, that it was my brother who had started the whole thing and was doing something wrong. She shouted something, including for him to "Stop it!"; and I laughed to myself for a plan well executed. Now all I needed to ensure safety was to put on the innocent victim look and make it safely into the secure presence of my mother. Perhaps being the younger has some advantages, too.

Now I do have to give some credit to my brother, who having some sense of humor and godly mercy, gave me some points for creativity in this last plan for dealing with my disadvantages. For in the end, he did not make me pay too much when mom and dad weren't around. I do have to say that I love my brother still and am grateful for the things he taught me.

Thanks, Jor.
Love,
Jon

My First Trip to the Dentist . . . in Russia

I had been dragging my feet, hoping that the pain in my tooth would go away. It had all started a few months before when I bit into something hard and that pain, which shoots through all the bones in your body, causes you to involuntarily close your eyes as a means of coping and holding on to consciousness, and forms that small tear-drop in the corner of your eyes, did its thing. I was hoping that it was nothing serious and that it was a near miss. However, as time went on, the pain began to reoccur with less and less pressure being applied to that tooth. I thought I had fractured the tooth, and it was only a matter of time before I would have to have something done. My initial hope was that I could hold out until we were back in the States, and I could listen to music through the CD player and headphones while my dentist went to work on me.

Unfortunately, the pain began to appear even in the context of eating a piece of bread (with butter to soften it even more—medicinal amounts only).

So with a lot of anxiety, I set off towards the dental industry here in hopes that the facilities, service and hygiene would be adequate for the situation at hand. I traipsed (as if mere walking wouldn't do) to the old, though newly painted, wooden building not far from my house. The internal corridors and doors with worn wood and chipped paint from the ten or so layers that had been applied over the years gave the impression of stepping back in time to the 1940s and 1950s. I found this of particular interest, since I was born in the 1960s and would not really know what the 40s and 50s were really like. Yet my imagination gave me the impression that this is precisely what it would have been like back then. Is that strange? Perhaps I've been in Russia too long.

I found the registrar and set up an appointment for that afternoon (oh fortunate me). Later, just before my appointment, I wanted to clean and brush my teeth to put on a good show for the dentist. (This is kind of like when my mom used to have a cleaning lady come over, and all of us kids had to clean and straighten up beforehand . . . it still doesn't make sense to me.) Upon flossing (following dental and parental advice), I popped half of my tooth off in my mouth. I started to get that strange, queasy feeling in the pit of my stomach. I examined the remains of the tooth both in my hand and in my mouth. It didn't look good. It broke, not vertically, but horizontally; and there was not much of a tooth above the gum line. Apparently, the "hopefully non-existent" crack had worked its way across the tooth. I felt I was now committed; but to what, we would have to wait and see.

I finished brushing, grabbed the remains of the tooth and headed down to the dentist's with more of everything: fear, anxiety and prayer. (I even sat down with Sasha to pray before I went—he was pretty comforting . . . praying for protection and safety and then somehow it trailed into thanking God for all the toys he had, and his bed, etc. . . .)

The equipment in the dentist's office looked fairly

modern and perhaps even Finnish in origin. My mood started to pick up. The dentist (a robust woman with dark black bushy hair) directed me toward the chair. As I started to try to explain the situation and hold up the remains of my tooth, she pressed me down into the chair and tipped my head back with her hands and began her examination. It appeared she wanted to do an assessment of all of my teeth and not just deal with the situation at hand (or the remains of which was in my hand at the time). So, I let her. I didn't really have a choice.

I earnestly tried to find out what she was planning to do about the immediate tooth problem; and apparently, the other teeth that she seemed to find equally amusing. Not much later, it became painfully clear that there were two additional teeth that she wanted to do something with the following day.

Pressing her for details was like pressing against concrete. I am sure that whoever came up with the phrase "butting your head against a brick wall" had her in mind. She was the dentist and I was not. (In Russia there doesn't seem to be anything called "patient's rights," except for in the phrase, *"You're the patient, right?!!"*) With this particular *woman/dentist* (the jury was still out on both counts), it was as if once you were in her office, you left all rules behind governing reality and civilized society and now had to submit to *"The All Authoritative and Ruling Witch,"* and no amount of clicking of slippers would save you. It's just that I was used to a little more "patient care" and good bedside manner back home. Although I wouldn't say she purposely tried to scare or threaten me, I wouldn't say she did much to calm my fears either. It also seemed I could not get any further clarification on what she was about to do other than give me a shot—which I hoped to God was just Novocain.

Feeling like I had no way out with my tooth in my hand, I rested my head back on the chair and continued to offer up non-verbal prayers. All the while, she had this habit of curiously grabbing my head and jaw and moving it this way and that—much like a grandmother on pension who is picking out a good melon—with much prodding and handling. She did not ask me once to hold my head a certain way or turn it this way or that . . . she told me to do it, and scolded me if I didn't hold it just right.

At this particular time, I found myself a little hesitant to ask for the CD player and headphones that I had grown so accustomed to in the States. Something nagging at me inside, or perhaps tugging on me on the outside, held me back. Perhaps it was the unselfish thought that they just might only have one set of headphones and maybe another patient, in more pain than I, would have a greater need for it. Or quite possibly it was the fear of being called a "sissy" and having to deal with the fact that I had been pampered in the dental world since birth. The last reason, buried deeply somewhere in my subconscious, was that I would get this strange look from them if I even broached the subject, and then tortured and treated as if I were from some other planet and couldn't speak their language. For whatever the reason, I went without it.

Without boring you by going into all of the details of the operation, I will cut, as it were, to the chase. Although at this time, I am reminded of my childhood when, upon experiencing a loose tooth, my creative and sometimes spontaneous father attempted the old *"string attached to the door knob"* trick to remove said tooth, and the first "slam" was unsuccessful. (Oh, I'm sure you can imagine the pain, and perhaps some of you are even wincing experiencing it sympathetically and empathetically right now). Of course, you might also be able to visualize the frightened and fearful look on my face and in my eyes, pleading that we try something else. And not just that we try it from the other direction of opening the door fast instead of closing it. Though not verbally offered, it seemed like that thought crossed my father's mind at the time. (Someday, I will have to tell you about my father and the old "dragging the ski boot across a carpeted floor" trick.) I begged off further experimentation and remained with my tooth until at dinner, I bit into an apple, jarred it free, and proceeded to swallow it before I realized what happened.

Now, many years later in Russia, after what seemed an eternity, though only about 40 minutes in real time, the Russian woman dentist (one out of three isn't bad) glued a new tooth in place. And for fear that it wouldn't hold, she glued it to the surrounding teeth as well.

Well, some time has passed; and it is now the second day and after my second visit. You might find yourself asking, "Why on earth did he go back?" Quite simply, she told me to. Don't laugh. Had you seen her, you would have done the same and had as much difficulty as I did trying to keep your voice from sounding like a young boy going through puberty when replying, "Yes ma'am." She also made it very clear that she really wanted to go at the tooth another time, and this time, do it right. Now by "doing it right," she meant taking off what she had done before, drilling out the nerve, and putting a post in to have something to support a new tooth.

I have until next Tuesday before this heralded event. I am seriously pondering whether to go ahead with it or, if at all possible, wait until we head back again to the States sometime around early May. Anyway, I wanted to share just some of the small day-to-day things that we encounter here in order to do the work God has, at this time, called us to. To be continued . . . .

On Teeth and Heroes

We have so many heroes who have become an inspiration to us all and have challenged us and called us to go beyond ourselves and rise to greater heights than we thought possible.

> ●Our Founding Fathers, who endured great conflict and fought for a Constitution that would provide equal rights for all men and religious freedom.
> ●Sports heroes in basketball, soccer, football, etc..., and also in the Olympics.
> ●Even cartoon and comic book heroes: the race car drivers; the robots and those who control them; the superheroes, those from other planets or changed by them; and those childhood heroes who made us dream of being able to fly, do amazing things and have incredible super powers.
> ●And then there are those great Biblical figures listed in Hebrews chapter 11—those heroes of faith...

Abraham, who believed God, began a nation through which Christ would come. Figures like Moses who faced the King of Egypt and stood fast in the deliverance of his people, and David who felled Goliath. Daniel who endured the lions' den without harm, and his friends who lived after being thrown into the fire without being burnt or even a hint of smoke on them—even though those who threw them in died because of the intense heat of the fire.

It is in times of trials and challenges that we can look at their lives of striving and hard work, faithfulness and commitment, and gain strength to endure whatever is in front of us.

Regarding my tooth and the Russian root canal surgery that I was facing, I chose to draw my role model from a particular knight whose story is retold in a British film in search of that sacred object. For this particular knight, when faced with a difficult and ferocious challenge, ran away.

And so dear friends, it is as I have chosen. Having been able to even eat meat with the temporary replacement/fix that the dentist applied on the first day, I have decided to put off the root canal until further notice of pain and/or circumstance.

Gratefully yours,

Jon

P.S. I hope that by this example, I haven't caused you great disappointment or discouragement in reaching new heights or facing tough challenges in relationships and the world around us. Further, I hope that it has not caused you to lose all hope and faith in me. Please rest assured that at the next earliest possible convenience, I will throw myself to the lions with a shout of "follow me!" coming from my lips.

P.P.S. For all of you who are not familiar with or fond of British humor, please forgive the brief reference.

P.P.P.S. The following note was sent out not long after . . . .

Hey folks,
Just wanted to let you know I have another dentist appointment tomorrow. The temporary fix didn't work out.

So what this means is that I am bound for something resembling drilling through teeth, nerve extraction *(author's note: the word, "extraction" is rarely used in a positive context)*, and "testing the Lord" tomorrow.

Now, some might not be familiar with the whole notion of *testing the Lord*, but it has something to do with doing something foolish or outside of the clear promises of God, and yet hoping or trying to force God to act in order to save you from the consequences. One example of this is say, jumping off a building and then, on the way down, asking God to rescue you because He loves you. Another example of this was every time I rode the large scenic-view carousel on the lakefront in Petrozavodsk. Taking into account the location of the carousel, the visual clues of rust everywhere, and the audio backup of creaking and grinding, I found myself always thinking, "I am a fool for getting on this thing again, and this is indeed, testing the Lord."

So as luck would have it regarding my dental discomfort, I found myself going against all reason and inclinations of the Spirit, and heading for what many conservatives might label as *testing the Lord*. Jumping off a cliff might be a safer bet.

The next chapter in the saga won't be written until it's over. So stay tuned as once again, our hero travels back in time to bring history to life.

We now return you to one of your regularly scheduled programs:

One Day in the Life of Ivan Dentistovich

(not to be confused with the book of similar sounding title)

Though may be found under these other possible subtitle headings:

"Tooth Scapades" (as offered by a long-time friend)
"101 Better Things to do with Your Time"
"It Could've Been Worse" (Sequel to **"A Better Movie with a Better Title"**)
"New Uses for Your Power Drill"
or my favorite,
"My Date with the Bride of the Creation of a German Scientist on the Edge" **(My Third Encounter of the Dental Kind)**

We pick up our story as I step back in time and re-enter the painted, wooden building again and make my way down the hall towards the dentist's room. My journey takes an immediate turn as I learn that, due to remodeling, the wardrobe room (as is customary in most Russian establishments of any kind, you must hang your outer wear in a place removed from where you gather to eat, attend the theater, or visit hospitals or dentists, or public officials, and/or public services offices etc. . . .), is now located in the basement. My heart sank a little as I was hoping this wasn't an ill omen of some sort as to the direction of things about to take place.

Having left my coat with the attendant in the basement, I headed back upstairs to see what Fate and or God had in store for me . . . .

One hour later.

Truthfully, it was actually a lot less painful than I expected. And the dentist (she?) only yelled at me one time for moving my head—which, as God is my witness, I did not do. *She* was doing all of the moving around, prodding, poking, drilling, and fussing. After which, she showed me the little nerve that she extracted/pulled out. (I won't describe it in any more detail as it still gives me the willies. If curious, just ask your local dentist.)

As an aside, my friend Sasha, who helps me with language practice, said that when he had to have this done at the "free clinic," they drilled a little hole in the bad tooth, put arsenic in it, and then capped it again. Then after a day or so the nerve dies on its own—*not too surprising considering the arsenic bit*. Perhaps what is more of a surprise is that the patient survives. So apparently, when you go to the "pay clinic," as I chose to do, they do away with the arsenic bit—which I was very glad to find out. Whoever said that, "money doesn't buy happiness" didn't have arsenic as the alternative.

Well, after she showed me the nerve, she went to work on the post. It took her and her assistant about 15 minutes to

21

find the right size post that would fit the hole. It looked a lot like the many times I rummaged in my basement, garage, kitchen junk drawer or my toolbox hunting for that particular screw or bolt from the hoards that I had saved that would just come in handy when I needed it. (And I *"used to"* save just about everything. In fact one friend of mine accused me of being the type to save even the cord off of the old toaster oven. I remember telling him quite plainly, that "no, I did not save the cord to my old toaster oven, but rather the entire old toaster oven itself—just in case there was a part I might need later, including the cord.")

Anyway, I only felt a little nervous when I heard the words "going to have to saw it off," but was relieved to find that they were referring only to the post. However, I became very nervous when I heard several pieces hit the floor behind me. I hoped that the piece that was going to end up in my mouth wasn't one of them; or if it was, that they would at least have the decency to wipe it down with alcohol first.

She lightly hammered (*tapped is inaccurate here*) and cemented the post in and gave it a little time to set. Just as I thought the worst was over and that we were finally done, she then informs me that I am going to have to run, not clear across town, just under a half a mile, to get another x-ray taken of the tooth to make sure that the post made it all the way down. She warned me that there was no other way to be sure and so save the tooth.

So off I ran, down to get my coat from the basement and out into the drizzly day over the melting ice and mud from the last few days. I made it to the polyclinic fine—handed in my coat and ran up to the x-ray lab to await my turn. Luckily there wasn't that long of a line. I eventually had my x-ray taken. I then had to run downstairs again to pay for it. Then back up to get my x-ray, and then back down to get my coat and head back to the dentist.

I got back to my dentist's building and headed down to the basement to hand in my coat. This time the old man made some slight derogatory comments regarding my frequency of turn-in and withdrawal of aforementioned items. I refrained from saying something, only thinking to myself, "I am not the only one responsible for this situation we both find ourselves in . . . hmm?" And headed up to the dentist, hoping and praying that the x-ray would show everything is okay for I didn't want to find out about the "or else."

As God would have it (and thanks to all your prayers), the post is in and down to where it needs to be—according to her. Now the only remaining tricky part!?! I have to go back in tomorrow morning for the tooth part to be put on the post. For several reasons, some clear, some not so clear, I have to wait until tomorrow to complete this experience. And for the interim, I am left with a small metal post sticking out of one tooth and the caution from the dentist: "only eat on the other side of your mouth." Now, doesn't that sound easy?

If she thinks I am going to do anything or eat anything that may jeopardize this work to date, she doesn't really know just how far I am willing to go to *not* repeat this type of excitement again. I am prescribing myself a liquid fast until tomorrow.
Till then dear friends,
So long for now,
Jon

P.S. Just in case you were waiting for it and missed it, having left the dentist for the last time of the day, I ran down to the basement, got my coat, and headed home.

In Defense of the Fatherland?!?

Well, today is one of those days that, on the grand scale of things, will go down in the books as just a typical, unimportant day. A day that was occupied by the business of the obligations we are faced with in life. Of course, for some, this day might be very significant: whether that is due to overwhelming joy of a wedding or anniversary or perhaps the experience of sorrow through loss or tragedy. This is not meant, in any way, to reduce the meaning of the impact and importance of this day. It is a small attempt to draw up what could be a typical, drab day for others into the limelight of significance, if perhaps for only a few minutes.

Today was the 22nd of February. The place: a small city of 300,000 in the northwest corner of Russia. The events that took place actually occurred, and the names of the people involved have not been changed to protect the innocent, they have been omitted altogether for the sake of artistic license and undue embarrassment.

The day began with the fulfillment of a promise to a little boy to return to his kindergarten and celebrate with him, one of those father and son things. Only here in Russia, that just happens to be the celebration of the "Defenders/Protectors of the Fatherland/Native Land" (actual day of celebration is the 23rd of February—this was an advanced attack since many children would not be there the following day). Now for some, that might not raise an eyebrow as they might miss the potential irony here. For in this story, this particular father just happened to be an American. So you may begin to see the smile on this father's face as he is settling himself down in the small kindergarten room, on the small bench with other fathers and grandfathers and a few mothers and substitute relatives, in preparation for the festivities to begin. Feeling slightly out of place and not wishing to draw much attention, he tried to look the part of a proud father and fellow native to the country.

What followed was typical, I guess, for most kindergarten performances: some songs, games and your usual dose of silliness in the fanfare of it all. And, of course, there are always those few children who seem to not be in sync with others, easily distracted and even perhaps jumping around drawing slightly more attention to themselves. This father's son was one of them.

The children were attired in little ascots of blue and white providing the image, as it was intended, of little sailors in uniform. Two teams were formed, with the children described as if they were the crew of two different ships: The Brave and The Fast. And the competition and fun began. This would have been okay had not the attention and focus then turned to the fathers in the room to also participate in the day's festivities and competition.

Now it needs to be said, that this particular American father had never served in the military. He did pay his taxes, of course (*well most of them anyway*), and he had worked in the scientific field, lending a hand to certain projects that were tied to the safety and protection of his country. But apart from that, other than verbal, this was about all the defending of his country he had ever done. In fact, if the truth were known, this father in his early college days registered for the draft (as was legally required then) as a conscientious objector. It wasn't due to an overwhelming sense of fear or wimpiness. It was more due to the fact that this particular father, at that particular time, was an atheist. And so thought and believed that this life is all we had and that after it, that was it. With no promise of an afterlife, you were gone. And (as my father used to say) "as if to put a fine point on it," you would not know you were gone either or that you were ever here at any point in time in the first place. You would cease to exist. You would not be able to tell those who you loved and cared about and who raised you that you loved them.

So you see, to this father (though not a father at that time) to go off to war and get yourself killed, for whatever reason, seemed like a pretty silly idea. I understood that there might be some situations and circumstances that would have warranted fighting, like defending those you love and for freedom; but at that time, America was peaceful and our lives were fairly sheltered from some of the harsher realities of life that existed in other countries. So nothing seemed urgent and pressing to sign up and die for. His patriotic quote and cry of that day, would have only been, "I regret that I have only one life."

Back to the present at the kindergarten, the competition turned to such events as the sack race, tug-o-war, and searching for plastic bowling pins while blindfolded. Doing his best for his team against all odds, the father managed to regain several points that were lost by other fathers and surrogates for the day to bring the final score to an even four to four. Then there was the presentation of the awards where this father's son received the medal: "To the Clever, Fast and Courageous," followed by the obligatory-for-all participation in the Russian version of that infamous song where you are putting certain body parts in or out and moving them in a very undignified manner, called in Russia "Boogy Woogy, OK!" Now, for some, the very endurance of this song in any language may be likened to a sacrifice, making an alternative of hot pokers in the eyes sound appealing. For others, well I don't know, I haven't found any over the age of eight . . . .

At the end, all of the fathers or their substitutes received a card that wished each one a "Happy Defender of the Father Land/Native Land day!"

So this father and son took the trolley-bus home (they didn't walk since it was -25^C or -13^F). Proud because they both had: endured harsh weather conditions, hopped in a sack, pulled their weight, and crawled across the floor blindfolded, all for the good and glory of defending *their* native land. *Not to mention the shameful participation in* "Boogy Woogy, OK!"

Yours truly,

Ivan Davidovich

Now, for the record, later on in his college career/life, the father (though still not a father at the time) did indeed discover that God really does exist and that there is an afterlife for all who trust in Him through His Son. And so he finally found something worth dying for, and not only that, but worth living for as well. But that is another story . . . .

Hemorrhoids and Heartaches

According to the information bulletins on the wall in the Russian hospitals, 80% of the population suffers from some form or other of these pains in the ass. This malady is called the ailment of the civilized or intellectual, presumably because we are sitting more on our hind ends thinking about doing something rather than actually outside doing it. And apparently, whatever notions or ideas we come up with are for others to put in motion or to act out. So, who is really the intellectual here?

It seems also heavily connected with our diet and Einstein's law of conservation of mass and energy: $E=MC^2$. In other words, for the common, uncivilized and non-intellectual man: *"what goes in must come out."* Thus, if you put more massive things in, you must therefore exert more energy in order to get them out. And since "space" isn't conserved, it is one of the first things to go.

Now, knowing that more people suffer from this ailment does not really reduce the suffering and pain, though misery loves company. It may however reduce some of the shyness, shame and timidity in talking about it. As they say in Latin "Ergo, I go and you go" and "Not you too Brutus?" . . . hence this letter.

Now with regard to the pressing subject of hemorrhoids:

why then, if so many people suffer from them, aren't we willing to drop the walls and drawers here and talk and share more openly? You know, like, "Hey Tom, Richard or Harry how are your hemorrhoids today? "Just fine. Thanks for asking."

And what could possibly be worse than hemorrhoids? (Oh yes, we are back to elephant jokes . . . .) . . . Having them in Russia . . .

If you thought that going to the doctor in Russia was something uncomfortable . . . .

Well, we have an unwritten policy on our team where we issue a gun to each team member. This is in case there is an emergency requiring hospitalization, and we are still conscious and in full use of our faculties. For all those other situations: may God be with you.

Then, there are those other situations that arise where adventure seekers who want to push the envelope on the word "thrill," chance the outpatient examination for a problem or two that just can't seem to wait the two or three years before we go back to the States.

(Now in all fairness, my wife did undergo an emergency appendectomy in Russia, which did indeed save her life. They really did a superb job. However, much if not all of her modesty was removed from her as well as her appendix. It actually happened the day before we were to leave for the other side of Russia, six time zones away, where we were due to complete the adoption of our youngest son, and on the occasion of my wife's 40th birthday to boot. But, all of that is another story . . . .)

Now, I don't know who invented hospital gowns, the ones that tie in the back leaving your rear exposed, but it must have been a woman. For only women seem to have the necessary skill of being able to tie that properly behind their backs with some measure of closure. It may come from all the practice with their uh, hmm . . . *"vertical support."* In honest confession, the very first time I was handed one of those gowns and told to put it on, I did the most logical thing. I put the opening in front, crossed it over like a bath robe and tied it, and waited there proudly for whatever misfortune that would come my way. Only to be told by the attending nurse that I had put it on backwards. Feeling rather humiliated as if I was the butt end of a joke, I hesitatingly corrected the situation, though not with a great deal of success.

To this day, I still think there is a secret trick to it. Like tying it first and then throwing the whole thing over your head like a t-shirt or a dress. Or again tying it first and turning it around without putting your hands in the sleeves until you've completed your turning of the gown and have come to a complete stop. No one in the hospital industry will ever give you advanced instruction. I think they must have this running inside joke to see how patients cope with the impossible or no-win situation. I can hear the nurses now saying things like "Oh, you should see the patient in 104 . . . . And he only came in for an eye exam."
And, of course, no patient will ever share his inside knowledge and humiliating failures about the gown, since he or she never wants to admit publicly their difficulty with it. Just too embarrassing.

It's kind of like the time when I, as a young boy, found my mother's diaphragm and thought it was the biggest balloon type of thing I had ever found and tried to blow it up. The only thing that made that worse was that it was

Christmas Day, and all the rest of the kids were on our parent's bed waking them so that we could open the presents. It was at that particular moment that I chose to walk in, attempting to blow it up, and upon failing, asked, "What's this for?" (I did not at first and for many years comprehend their laughter . . . .) And once having understood it, realizing it is just not something you want to share openly with others . . . .

All that being said about the gowns, they do at least, in passing, provide some "false" sense of modesty to the patient, for sooner or later the gown is going to come off or be lifted up.

When I went in to "discuss" my problem with the doctor in Russia, this really wasn't a problem at all. No gowns. Just drop your pants and anything else you might happen to be wearing and get on the table. No false pretenses or facades of apparent modesty.

Now, I suppose it wouldn't have been so bad except for the middle-aged nurse who was also assisting and helping me up on the table and the fact that, at any time, any hospital staff or inquiring patient could stick their head in the door for whatever reason.

It's still a wonder to me, that I found myself in a cool hospital room near the end of winter more than half naked (for the optimist—less than half clothed) but sweating in anticipation. And praying of course—heck, I was already on my knees.

Now, what happened next, I can't really explain. Kind of like an epiphany of sorts and an ethereal detachment from the real world and the naked truth. I was carrying on a conversation with the nurse, and it didn't dawn on me until she left the room to get the doctor that I was buck naked talking to a complete stranger about this and that.

And as Adam and Eve did when they realized their own *situation*, I sought to cover myself by pulling down the front of my shirt. Thank God I wore one of the XL ones that day. Now, I also realized it was a little late for the nurse's sake, or mine, but just in case anyone else walked in . . . .

When the doctor walked in, I began to sweat a little more. He wasn't the type to smooth talk the patients and ease their frame of mind. He was of the "let's get down to business" kind while all the time telling me to relax. The snapping of the gloves onto his hands just made it worse. Nor did the realization help that I actually knew the doctor from before having played basketball with him. Not only did I regret his having big athletic hands, but all of those times I, inadvertently (and not) fouled him . . . I was praying that he was a forgiving man.

After some investigation with me lying on my side, they had me attempt to get on all fours and force my body into a position more suitable for an advanced yoga class. My body is just not made to bend that way. Especially, when I am naked and there is a doctor and nurse behind me telling me to relax. What was going through my mind was a role reversal of sorts, and I wanted to shout out, "Why don't you lie on the table, and I'll put on the gloves and tell you to relax!"

The doctor grabbed some device and talked to the nurse about needing to pump it up. I was more worried than before. In the States, when I had an examination of this nature, all I remember is telling the nurse after she gave me the IV that my arm was tingling. The next thing I knew, I was waking up in a completely different room, under covers

33

and semi-clothed in one of those reassuring hospital gowns.

Here, I had none of those hopes, especially about waking up somewhere else. More prayer was needed . . . .

Thank God it didn't last that long. The doctor left, and the nurse stayed to clean up as I got dressed. And just to put a thankful note in my heart, just as I was zipping up, a young, beautiful nurse came unannounced into the room and, holding the door open to the hall, asked about getting help from the older nurse for something or other.

Now, two surprising unexpected things came out of that adventure.

The first being: the older nurse, as soon as I was finished dressing, came up and asked me in sincerity about my faith. (Some of that must of have come out earlier in talking to the doctor or while I was in my happy place while they were torturing me on the table.)

Of course, all of my manly images, comparing myself to great warriors like the heroes in many battle movies, were quickly dashed when I realized that something so small as a hemorrhoid was enough to bring me to my knees and give out the location of the buried treasure.

She started by asking "if it was possible for her, a person with one foot in the grave, to really have a belief in God after all that time has gone by?" And, "did I really, honestly believe in God and was I sure about it?"

I laughed inwardly and muttered something mentally to God as it seems that He has his own sense of humor in the divine appointments He makes for us. I shared with her just briefly my own history of being an atheist until I was 22. And then, after some study and investigation, I told God that I was 51% sure He still didn't exist, but on the 49%, I wanted what He had to offer. And that by now, I was fully convinced by God Himself of His existence and personal presence in my life. (And what I didn't share of course was: what other reason could you possibly give for an American to willingly be found in the far northern parts of Russia, with his pants down, lying on an examination table? This is clearly all God's doing. And when I see Him . . . .)

The second surprise was that my "thorn in the flesh" seemed to go away almost from the day of the appointment. Now, all the doctor really did was to prescribe a change of diet and some cream. But the results happened before I really put any of that into practice. So, again I am left pondering two thoughts: one is that God, in His sense of humor and appointments, really wanted me to talk to that nurse; which I can accept and actually be thankful for . . . in the end.

The other is that: between my mind and my body, we convinced each other that something needed to change because we *NEVER* want to have to go through that again! And this time, my body and mind agreed whole heartedly.

Scare tactics. How is that for the latest in hemorrhoid treatment?

Hope this helps,

Yours....

Jon

I Can't Believe It. My Mother was Right.

(The following observations contain language that may be unsuitable for the more sensitive reader, children under five or highly conservative Christians who may have a problem with the use of the word "ass" or any of its derivatives. These observations are not meant or intended to cause any offense at all; rather, they are an attempt to more accurately describe or explain what we, in reality, observe and experience.)

Years growing up, my mother always believed that most ailments could be treated with a thorough cleansing of your system, which meant plenty of fluids and an enema. From the common cold to headaches to just plain feeling blah, all could just be flushed down the toilet, so to speak.

And since that was her belief, it became part of our growing up experience. No, I am not complaining. Nor will I come out with a book entitled, "What I Endured at the Hands of My Mother" or "How Mom Could Be a Real Pain in the Ass." For in fact, this procedure, whether coincidental or otherwise, seemed to actually work . . . sometimes.

However, in trying to explain this today in the modern world of science and medicine to some of our friends, I am met with laughter, some skepticism, and even the *fleeting*

36

thought of child abuse. To them, giving your child an enema for a headache seems to be archaic, a folk myth, or at the very least "back-asswards." To them, it seems rather obvious that if your head is hurting, you should work more in that area of the body and take your choice of aspirin, acetaminophen, or ibuprofen instead of going south for your answers. For how on earth could shoving something up your rear end make your head feel any better? Unless, of course, the relief of its removal far exceeded the "uncomfortableness" of putting it there in the first place, would there be some justification for even attempting this procedure. And that, of course, is really what this whole theory of medicine is based upon.

Though, I am sure the first person to ever try this was more than a little hesitant about the whole idea. "You mean what?? Where do you want to me to put this thing? You've got to be kidding." And finally, "Come hell or high water!. . . ." *(And probably receiving both).* And I wouldn't doubt at all that, given the history of man and medicine, he might not have even been a paid, willing participant. To put a fine point on it, my one sister offered, from her knowledge of history and certain religious practices, that certain monks put the two words "suffering" and "gourd" together. I will leave that to your imagination; and let you know that, in this context, one of those words is used in both the noun and gerund-verb form.

Now, in fairness and respect to my mother, she was also a "victim of circumstances" having grown up with her mother and father who strongly believed in natural approaches to medicine. From what I hear, in fact, her father was brilliant man, a physician and author, often referred to in many family stories as "Doc." It is with real pain, grief and sadness that my mother talks about him to me since she had a deep longing for me to have met him and him to have seen me. Unfortunately, he died just before I was born. I, too, feel a sense of loss when I hear about him and would have liked to have gotten to know the man who had such an unconscious influence on my life.

He was, as it turns out, indirectly and partly responsible for my life, *for if it weren't for him, my mother would have been a totally different person or perhaps not a person at all.* I really like how Warren Miller put it: "If your parents didn't have children, odds are you won't either."

My mother's mother, my "Gramma Emma," was a feisty old woman who would insist that all of her grandchildren play "Casino" with her. ("Casino" is a fun card game that can easily be played with just two players). It really wasn't so bad. But you had to watch out for Grandma. She would occasionally do things that were "outside the rules of the game." "Cheating," though, would not be a fair word to use since you were never quite sure if she was doing it on purpose or because she had poor vision. Regardless, she won more games than she lost. She enjoyed relating to others and loved to be among her peers stirring up life in them, even if she was at times cantankerous and feisty. She lived to be 93.

I still remember how I used to tease her by patting her on the head and then grabbing and pulling her hair. *(Just another something I learned from watching another British comedy growing up).* She would make a few swinging attempts at me in play, but my arms were long enough by then to keep well out of her reach. Ahhh, I remember those tender expressions of love that we shared . . . especially when

38

my folks went out of town and left Gramma in charge . . . or us in charge of Gramma. It really wasn't clear; it seemed to be more of a peer relationship.

Anyway, on this occasion, I was not yet 21 and wanted to have a few of my friends over for a little party while the Ps were away. So, I, in my cleverness, convinced Gramma to come with me to buy some beer for us. *(No, wait, it gets better.)*

I drove her to the local liquor store, and I am trying to play the part of the helpful grandson, helping grandma pick out the best case of beer. I am sure you can imagine the picture. Trying to appear that we were working together, examining the prices and making the selection took no small amount of acting and clever misdirection. I mean like, grabbing the case of beer, holding it up a little and examining it for any defects and "appearing" to be holding it for Gramma's inspection. I even nodded my head as if in agreement to her choice. *(Again most British humor fans know that any facial or head gesture is as good as another; and so it was in this case, that any acknowledgment of my actions from my Gramma was taken as an affirmative.)* I put the case of beer in the cart, and we moved on to the checkout. Though to try to remove suspicion further and to draw less attention, instead of just rushing to get in and out of the store, I guided her slowly through the aisles, stopping occasionally to pick up a bottle of something and examine the price. All the while, trying to make it look like I wasn't afraid, but rather that I was *browsing* in a sophisticated manner and indeed had all the rights to be there.
I might have even grabbed some other items along the way that we didn't need just to throw the scent more off the trail.

What I do remember quite clearly is that at the checkout, while trying to draw as little attention as possible and have Gramma actually hand the money to the cashier, I sort of quickly stuffed some cash in Gramma's hand and told her to pay for the purchase. Slightly puzzled might best describe the look on the cashier's face; worried on mine. And as for Gramma, the jury was still out, though she still handed him the money. As he handed her back the change, I thought we were home free and so started to push the cart a little forward and even nudge her from behind. However, Gramma was in front and she wasn't moving. She held the change clenched in one fist and waved it at the cashier and then demanded to know if it included the "senior citizen's discount." I could feel the cold sweat starting around my temples and inside my shirt. It would only be later that I would be able to look back on that and laugh. Only Gramma Emma.

So that is what my mother grew up with.

Now, much, much later in life, in Russia, sitting in bed with my wife reading and discussing what remedies there were for clearing up sinus infections apart from using antibiotics all the time, I came upon this section in the book entitled, Back to Eden, by Jethro Kloss.[1] I would like to quote it, however to avoid legal problems I'll put it in my own words, though the recognition belongs to him.

On treatment of sinus problems:
He recommends getting rid of the sources of the problem.

---

1   Kloss, Jethro. 1994. *Back To Eden, New Revised Edition, & 55th Anniversary Edition*. Back to Eden® Publishing Co.
**Reproduced with permission from *Back to Eden*, by Jethro Kloss, Lotus Press, a division of Lotus Brands, Inc., PO Box 325, Twin Lakes, WI 53181, USA, www.lotuspress.com © 1994 All Rights Reserved

Getting your system up and running so that you take one to three extensive trips to the bathroom a day, *AND* cleansing your system with a far-reaching enema. But the good news he saves for the last. He says this process could take *weeks."* *(Emphasis added)*

Now, the first step makes perfect sense and follows reasoning. If you have something clogging up your nose and nasal passages, get it out of there. Yet, it is the actual removal process that sounded more and more like my mother growing up. *I started to have that feeling on the back of my neck . . . and began to hear my mother's voice in my head.*

So, after doing what you possibly can about the sources of your sinus problems, the next step, which doesn't seem to follow the lines of deductive reasoning at all, can be distilled down to getting your system up and running and regular. Now regular can mean a lot of things, but only one in this context. So, we are talking about regular with a capital "R," and a "one to three times daily" associated with it. Now, the difficulty lies in the fact that the word, *Regular,* is a subjective term, and what is *Regular* to some just might not be enough of the *Regular* you are looking for to rid yourself of your sinus problem. You may, for the sake of a healthy example of *Regular,* need to look over at *old Jones* who seems to spend a lot of time daily in the bathroom, and who is able to complete, not only the important work at hand, but also the sport's page, the crossword, and one number puzzle too—meaning that some of those trips are fairly protracted, successful endeavors. Now, we are just warming up. Here is the part we've all been waiting for with much anticipation. After removing the source of the problem, and working yourself up to Regularity, it is now time to flush your system with an enema. *And you were wondering all this time what they were really for having passed them many times in the aisle at the pharmacy. Perhaps they were not in the Sinus Trouble area with the other decongestants?* It is probably important to note that this isn't just a regular enema we are talking about, *as if even one of them could be considered regular.* It is a far-reaching enema that is prescribed. And as if that weren't enough, the author of the book lets you know that this process could take *weeks.* *"Oh, crap!"*

Sitting up in bed, my first thought was, "my mother was right!?!" She has been saying this for as long as I can remember. In fact, many times her first question to us was not "How are you doing?" "How's the G.P.A.?" or "Do you have a temperature?" But instead, "How are your B.M.s?"

My second thought immediately following that was, "How can that possibly be???"

You mean to clean my sinuses, I have to cleanse my colon!?! That is one hell of a "far-reaching" enema if you ask me. Maybe this is where the saying "the proof is in the pudding" came from.

But by now, I am sure you can begin to see the justification, origination, and implications of many of our sayings and expressions that seem to carry more truth than we ever thought . . . . (a*nd where the rest of this letter is heading.*)

So the next time you hear someone say, "Hey buddy, get your head out of your ass," you can say, "I wish," and laugh quietly to yourself, knowing that he is closer to the truth than he could have ever possibly imagined.

Additionally, I would never have equated sinuses and

rear ends so closely together except in the previous references to someone's nose and its recent adoption of a brown tone.

Drawing the connections then, for the next time you want to be helpful at work, you can walk up to your boss, hand him or her an enema and, with all of the weight of medical science behind you, say, "Here, go get your head cleaned out."

Furthermore, whatever you may have been called with with word, *"head"* attached, or *calling into question what you have for brains or that you might, indeed, be sitting on them,* are also likely derivatives from this truth . . . for here it can be understood that they are not just names to call someone, but actually refer to a medical state or condition they may be experiencing. And *"Oh s#%t!"* is not just an expression in response to a sudden, unfortunate event but is also clearly derived from the medical field as a rhetorical question in response to finally understanding, and restating the solution to our problems explained to us by the doctor. Patient's reply, "Oh…, *s#%t*??!?"

On the opposite side of things, I do foresee the marketing problems for the enema manufacturers' new product line of "Anal-Nasal Spray"—especially the flavored ones. But now, "I'm so stuffed up" takes on a much fuller meaning.

Well, I just felt *moved* to put it in writing and say "Thanks, Mom, for bringing all these things to the surface." And without you none of this would have been possible.

Here are a few other implications and origin favorites of mine that make so much better sense now *taken in enema* context than they ever did:

43

- *"Hey, Doc, can you please remove your cuff links?"*
- *"Kindly remove your head from my rear, lower portions so that I can think."*
- *"Men only have one thing on their mind."* Well, that is because that member of our body is actually closer to the real source of our problems and headaches than we ever thought before.
- *"What goes in must come out."*
- *"I am so happy, I could just have a bowel movement."*
- *"Relax, I've got your back covered."*
- *"Your problem is that you are so full of what you need to be rid of."*
- *"Oh, how long must I endure this?"*
- Nurse (x-ray tech) to doctor: *"Look out! The excrement is headed for the ventilation shaft."*
- *"Do unto others....period!"*
- *"Hold on, it's going to be a rough ride."*
  "Fasten your seat belts, we are encountering turbulence."
    &
- *"This time around, You tube Brutus."*

So Mom and Dad, you can argue as to whose son I am the product of. For you gotta wonder, *"What kind of guy writes about this kind of crap?"*
Finally, in passing..., alls well that ends well, and bottoms up . . . .!
Merry Christmas and a Happy New Year
Love, Jon

P.S. Look for enemas under the Christmas tree

My Conclusions

Dear Friends and Family,

A very dear friend asked me to explain why it was or how I could come, or must come (future tense), to the same conclusion that God is good and just despite the outcome of our current situation. I thought that was a valid and good question to share, with my response to all who have been with us in prayer, encouragement and support.

The current situation still whether or not we will have the joy of bringing Sasha home as our son, or watching him be sent to another orphanage for another four years with no possibility for adoption. The orphanage is not a prison, but it is a thin substitute for the love, care, and freedom that only a family can provide. For the last five years, Sasha's world consisted of a bedroom, a playroom/eating room, a changing room, and a small physical training room—all of which was shared with about ten other children at all times. On top of that, the courtyard to the orphanage was surrounded by a fence that amounted to the edge of the world for them, outside of which was a mystery much like in the days of Columbus.

We began to visit Sasha several months ago and take him for walks—all he wanted to do was go for long walks outside the fence and see what the rest of the world was really like.

He has a fascination and a curiosity as well as a fear for the strange new things he encounters. (He was very frightened by our vacuum cleaner and still is terrified by dogs). We had everything prepared for him at our home/apartment and had been, over the past three months, trying to explain the transition that would take place when he came home with us for good and live there instead of in the orphanage. That is why, when this whole process came to an unexpected halt, and perhaps an irreconcilable position from the biological parents, our hearts felt crushed and a sadness mixed with depression seemed to flood over us as if a river overran its banks and the dam burst.

Over the past several weeks, we have continued to meet and play with Sasha not knowing the outcome. At times we are "okay" as much as can be expected; and at other times, the sadness and depression make it almost impossible to even get off the couch. It is very difficult to know what to say to Sasha, as we still want to gather him in our arms and tell him that things will be okay and that "when he comes to live with us, we will . . . ." And just this past week, for the first time, when Mary was bringing him back to the orphanage after we took him to Tanya's to have tea and celebrate her birthday, he ran back to Mary and gave her a hug and said, "I really love you." Before this, he had responded at times to our verbal expression of our love for him by telling us that he loved one of the aunts at the orphanage. For at the time, his understanding seemed to be that he could only love one person at a time; and, of course, those childcare workers were the only adults in his life, save for the doctor and maintenance worker. We took him to the lakefront to see snow and ice sculptures, eat cotton candy and caramel popcorn—we took him to play hockey for the first time and bought him a mini hockey stick—we took him sledding with other friends of ours. Our hearts and lives were already joined, and the thought of losing him at times feels too much to bear.

So, how is it then that I can or must come to the conclusion that God is both good and just in the midst of this and regardless of the outcome?

It is not an attempt to ignore or repress the pain and sadness or to come off as some super spiritual Christian. In reality, this has been and continues to be one of the most difficult and sad times of our lives as we wait, not knowing the outcome. Like I said, sometimes we have felt we "couldn't punch our way out of a wet paper bag." Yet, at the same time, through this process, God is teaching us many things about ourselves, our selfishness, our weaknesses and our strengths, and a lot about Himself. We are being stretched beyond where we thought possible, and the fear is that we will snap as a rubber band that has reached its elastic limit. Perhaps being stretched is what God is after, or even "brokenness" if it breaks us from our selfish independence of Him, and the turning from false idols (all those silly and seemingly important things we turn to for deep satisfaction and true fulfillment, which often turn out to be only empty false hopes providing only a temporary sense of what we truly seek. Those things we think we must have in order to be happy, significant or fulfilled—all those things that are a poor substitute for God). This is what, in Jeremiah, God says:, *"For My people have committed two evils: They have forsaken Me, The fountain of living waters, to hew for themselves cisterns, broken cisterns, that can hold no water. "*[2] They left God and went after things that in the end could never truly satisfy their deep longings and thirst.

In addition, our guarantee, or promise that God gives us is not that he will give us what we want or remove our trials and struggles, but that He *"causes all things to work together for good to those who love God, to those who are called according to His purpose."*[3] Our trust, faith and hope is not in the outcome, nor is it in the strength of those things themselves—trust, faith and hope—for they are nothing in and of themselves. Our hope, trust and faith are truly dependent upon the object of which they rely. God is trustworthy. He fulfills His promises. He is both loving and just. And Christ Himself says "what man is there among you, when his son shall ask him for a loaf, will give him a stone?[4] . . . How much more shall your Father who is in heaven give what is good to those who ask Him." We are definitely and clearly asking and pleading with God that we will be able to adopt Sasha—not for our sakes alone, but for his and his future. Though it is quite clear we do have a personal stake in it. Whether this be through moving in the biological parents' hearts to allow Sasha to be adopted, or making a very clear and concise decision by the courts to see that Sasha be in the place where it may be best for him. (I am not thinking how great and perfect parents we will be and how we deserve this in comparison, etc. What we are saying

2   Jeremiah 2:13, New American Standard Bible®, Copyright © 1960, 1962, 1963, 1968, 1971, 1972, 1973, 1975, 1977, 1995 by The Lockman Foundation.
3   Romans 8:28 New American Standard Bible®, Copyright © 1960, 1962, 1963, 1968, 1971, 1972, 1973, 1975, 1977, 1995 by The Lockman Foundation.
4   Matthew 7:9, New American Standard Bible®, Copyright © 1960, 1962, 1963, 1968, 1971, 1972, 1973, 1975, 1977, 1995 by The Lockman Foundation

is that we are willing to accept the full responsibility for the love and care of Sasha. To live with the heartaches and pain as he grows up and experiences illnesses and difficulties and the joy of seeing him develop into a mature person understanding God's love for him.)

Now, having said that, it would be very easy to conclude and shout that God is good and just if we have Sasha as our son. If we don't get what we want or pray for, can we then conclude that God is not good, loving and just? We all know from experience what happens to those children who always get what they want or demand—they tend not to grow up well and are unprepared to handle difficult situations in life. If our heavenly Father does not give us what we want, His character hasn't changed any, nor His heart and desire for us. I know when I was a child, at times when my parents disciplined me *(rare for I was such a good child)* or did not give me what I wanted, there were times when I got angry and even shouted "I hate you." (My mom even at times would tell me that that was okay—that made it only more frustrating and confusing as it seemed somehow to take all the fun and steam out of it.) So, the reality of it is that our heavenly Father knows what is truly best for us. He loves us and desires to give to us. If we do not get what we want here, we will be heartbroken, saddened, and my guess is also angry at God. There may even be a time when literally or figuratively I shake my fist at him and for the moment say "I hate you." But, our Father's continual love and embrace comforts us as we work through our anger and sobbing; and if we wrestle through it and choose not hold onto selfish bitterness, we will experience more deeply our relationship with Him and know truly just how much he cares for us.

49

There is one other aspect about this situation that helps to bring my eyes upward and that is that others are experiencing similar suffering or maybe more severe, and yet they are still pursuing God and coming to the same conclusion about their heavenly father. Many have lost children or spouses through accident or illness or through wars, both of merit and without.. Many are wrestling through illnesses now that, save for an intervention by God, will most likely result in death in the near future. One such person is Katya. She is young—mid 20s, beautiful, married and has two children. Just this past summer, she began to attend some of our studies. Since then, she has entered into a relationship with God and is as hungry and excited to learn as much as she can. She helps out in one of the children's music studies and with our larger gathering of folks, as well. She regularly attends several studies a week and was even a little disappointed that the women's advanced group, which she just started attending, only meets every other week. You can see in her a joy and love for God. She also is battling cancer, and depending upon its extent, the care and treatment here, only God knows how long she has. I thank God for her and also pray for her healing as well. But, whether He heals her or whether we get to adopt Sasha or not, we do have *now* the opportunity to know His love and to share that with others, and what a precious opportunity that is.

No, God isn't fair. In fact, He gives us far and beyond what we deserve. In a world separated and alienated from Him—bearing the full consequences and deserving judgment, He offers us, individually, a free gift of forgiveness, eternal life, and the opportunity to be his ambassadors and fellow workers in helping reconcile mankind back to Him. As if that weren't enough, our relationship with Him is not based on our performance, but on our adoption into His family and household so that we can call out to Him—"Dad," and know that He loves us in the fullness of that relationship. Our sons may be disobedient, go their own way, and even hopefully someday leave the house, but despite their actions that I may like or dislike, they will always be our sons. That is what our relationship is like with our heavenly Father. I have more than enough. I have more than I deserve.

What other conclusion could I come to?

Thanks for your ears and time in helping me work through this. Love, Jon

My Sister the Clown-Maker

I really do not remember how old I was. Though it must have been somewhere between the ages of four and seven because I don't have too many memories of before that time and only spotty ones during that age of my life. (Perhaps for good reason, too . . . .)

Take my eldest sister. It seems she began at a much earlier age to express the swirling thoughts of the soul within her for after the moment that she learned to stand and walk, she began to draw on the walls of her room. Much to the surprise and shock of our mother, who was wrestling with the two notions of: (1) receiving and appreciating with joy the creative gift and expression of her first daughter, and (2) getting only slightly upset at the damage done to both paint and wallpaper. Having not been there myself, I can't say for sure how my mother actually handled the situation. It may have been more than her "mild to medium" response, which often began with the word "what," and was drawn out to express the degree of disturbance in her soul, to the point of where the "t" was almost lost by the time she gained her composure to finish the question. "Whaaaaaaaaaaaaat... are you doing?" (The larger number of "a's," the greater the disturbance). Sometimes for effect, she would also add our names after the "what" for a finer focus of energy and importance. And if she was too flustered, she would just run down the list of our names till she got to the one she wanted. *After being a parent, I know how that can happen.* Our father would either be the good cop or bad, depending upon the situation and seriousness of the crime, and the state of the individual brought in for questioning.

So, there I was, a lonely, unprotected child of about four . . . .

Dad, I think, was at work or out on errands and Mom was either upstairs or away from home. There I was, left all alone with my two sisters to be the object of their attention, early mothering, and creative playing. My brother, being smarter and faster than I (at the time anyway), seemed able to avoid winding up in situations like this. But as fate would have it, I found myself again as an unwilling participant.

You know how girls like to play with dolls, play make-believe, dress up and put on make-up, etc. Well, what do you have when you have a little brother and the parents are neatly out of the way? I'll tell you what. You have a living clothes-horse to dress up. You have one of those things that people use to make and form dresses but only more fun—this one tries to get away. You have a life sized Mr. Potato Head with moving parts.

I wouldn't say that I am scarred from this event that took place almost 37 years ago. But, one does have to wonder why it is that memories like these stick out and seem to last so long. Or, it could be due to the fact that after the girls were done, it was put down on film which then finds its way to light every now and again throughout the years. One of those images you try all your life to forget and, certainly, not to have shown to every girlfriend who came to visit.

They made a clown out of me, with loose clothing and red lipstick. Now, I do not actually remember who was the brains behind it; whether it was my eldest sister or the second one on the scene. I do think an argument can be made that the elder had more responsibility and thus, ultimately held the knife—or the lipstick in this case. However, both share the guilt in this matter and in the memory.

Now, I don't know about other men or young boys, but having lipstick put on made me feel just a little bit foolish. I can't imagine what goes through a woman's mind when she puts it on. But if it adds to her beauty and the inner sense of her femininity, can you imagine what it would do on the wrong sex?

Well, it seems we all made it out of that time of our lives okay. My eldest sister went on to become an artist, a musician and a teacher of both art and Yoga. She now uses blocks of wood, metal or stone instead of little brothers to create the images that swirl around her soul. No longer drawing on walls, she crafts landscapes and structures that bring humanity and nature together in creative harmony. She also writes and plays music to use words, chords and melodies as an expression of who she is in the fullness of her being and experiences. And now, she is teaching Yoga, which I've found to be a lot like an advanced game of Twister, only your other player is the floor,....and he usually wins.

And to think that 37 years ago, I helped to play a part in that. Well, I suppose it was worth it. Not bad when you really think about what roles we play in helping others find and discover themselves and their talents in life, especially for a four or seven year old. Kind of puts it all in perspective doesn't it?

I guess what I miss now are those special times when we are all back together again, playing music (they, not I), and having fun and being silly (still they, not I). Those times come a little fewer and farther between, as we are all developing new relationships, living and working far apart, building families of our own, and caught up being very busy (we never were much for watching too much TV). Even though we may have forgotten the lessons from felines, cribs, metallic ladles, small azure figures and celestial bodies, we can hold those *times* we are together more dear.

Now, regarding what impact or effect did being made a clown have on me, you might ask? (Some of my friends might say that I never stopped being one. Possibly . . . though I've, since gotten rid of the lipstick.) Apart from the many different nuances of influence on who I am, what both of my sisters gave me was a memory that would last a lifetime. Now, that is also pretty neat.

My thanks to you both, and Happy Birthday, Kimmer!!

Love, Jon & the rest of gang, Mary, Sasha and Jhenya

P.S. It came out later, after writing this that my eldest claimed to have no real part in the caper. But rather that Julie was the sole perpetrator and artist at the time. Now, this could possibly be true—as one of my early memories of Kimmer has her pictured lying in her room upstairs on the floor on her stomach reading a book. Then, there's the image of Julie standing in front of me, holding my face quite scrunched-upily, and applying the lipstick rather generously and far from my lips. Though the question remains: who took the picture with Julie and me in it? Perhaps, I ran upstairs to show Kimmer what Julie had done, and she grabbed the camera. Ultimately, it is my recollection anyway; and with age, comes responsibility, and proximity rules apply. At the same time then, if you want help getting dressed up, give Jules a call. She now spends most of her time dressing up for the stage, directing, or playing her violin.

The Case of the Significant Error

Is it possible that one error could affect the lives of so many? I think, unfortunately, we know the answer to that question by experience and history. There are, however, those unique times in the course of the human tragedy/comedy, where these errors or mistakes actually change people's lives for the better; and the significance of the error takes on a much greater importance and depth. In fact, that significance and importance grows far beyond the paper on which the error is recorded.

Let's, for example in this case, take a mistaken entry in the computer of a child's date of birth. On the one hand, it seems like a very small error in which the consequences would be hardly worth noting or getting disturbed about. Now, there might be long-term consequences: the what-ifs for instance, if this error affected the child's timing on when he or she could learn to drive, vote, drink (legally), or be drafted or forced into obligatory military duty. Here, you might run the risk of trying to know the future and even deciding that in some cases, it might actually turn out better if the child's age got him out of a bad (as seen by you) situation. You may begin to see the depth and significance then, of not only our errors, but our decisions, as well; which, in reality, we live with the consequences all the time. I suppose that when things turn out well, we might call that luck or foresight or even coincidence. For some who believe and trust in God, we might well see His hand in working behind the scenes throughout our lives, sometimes obviously and sometimes not.

In the rough cases, when things don't go so well, we might, by default, start blaming others for the situation we find ourselves in. Some might even take it up with God as to the unfairness of it all and start pointing the finger at Him. Perhaps, in too many cases, we are unwilling to admit our own responsibility for the situations we find ourselves in (sometimes repeatedly—especially in relationships).

I am getting slightly off the subject, though, and will try to curve us back to the original road.

In realizing the potential outcomes and significance of our decisions and mistakes, one possible result would be to live our lives in fear, being afraid to take risks, make serious decisions, or make mistakes. Without much discourse on the subject of fear, let us say that thanks to God's same promise, "God causes all things to work together for good, to those who love God . . . .,"[5] we have a freedom to overcome fear, take more risks, and attempt to love others imperfectly (*though we might be prone to think "love imperfect others perfectly"*).

Now, back to the mistaken entry of the child's date of birth. This particular boy spent the first year and a half of his life in the hospital, struggling with many different illnesses, having barely escaped death in his first month and a half. The next four and a half years were spent in a Russian

---

5   Romans 8:28, New American Standard Bible®, Copyright © 1960, 1962, 1963, 1968, 1971, 1972, 1973, 1975, 1977, 1995 by The Lockman Foundation.

orphanage in the context of a group of ten other children. The borders of the orphanage were the edge of his galaxy, save for the several trips in the ambulance to the hospital over the years. He had biological parents, but due to the health concerns and distance, they felt they could not fully care for him and so had not seen him since a month after his birth.

Life in these orphanages varies, depending upon location, and sponsors that help supplement the deficiency in financial support from the government. This boy's orphanage was somewhat better in comparison for he had the loving care and attention of the director and many of the care-workers. Because of his previous illnesses, however, this boy would never find his way on to an adoption agency's list. In fact, he had already been turned down from the list and several would-be parents. When he turned five, he would be automatically transferred to an orphanage/school or *internat* for older children, where in truth, he would be consigned to live without hope of adoption. We had visited many of these older orphanages ourselves and had seen firsthand the numerous wonderful children who are practically unknown to the outside world. The local economic situation and culture does not promote or encourage the Russians to consider adopting older children. Therefore, often, these children grow up with a hope that eventually fades and that can, in some cases, lead to a very hardened heart, for the hope and longing for parents and a family never comes to pass. In addition, any hopes and dreams to achieve or become whatever that may be are out of reach due to the limited education and resources available.

In the course of events, due to this particular mistaken entry, the boy was allowed to stay in the first orphanage until he was discovered, accidentally, by a couple who had spent over ten years praying to have children. *(It turned out that the orphanage never received the orders to transfer him, since the ministry of adoption had his birth date as the date he entered the orphanage. In fact, up to that point, the error had not yet even been discovered.)* Now, here is where it gets even more remarkable. That particular couple had only been looking for children up to five years old. And according to their paperwork, they would never have been given permission by the local ministry to see this boy had the correct date of birth been known.

I think it may be fairly obvious by now to most of you who know Sasha and our history in becoming a family. What you may not have known is how significant that particular error played in Sasha's and our life and the joy that we have because of it. It is the "what ifs" that send a shudder through me and cause me to tear up when I think about what kind of life he would have had without that mistake. It is also that very same thing, which causes me to thank God from the depths of my heart and soul, for it is very clear to us that this has His handwriting all over it. Sasha just recently turned seven. This was his first birthday with us. It was during this time, that the significance of that error made itself felt.

With all our love,

Jon, Mary & Sasha

And now you know more of the beginnings of his continuing story . . . .

Travel Mercies

I don't even know where to begin this account . . . .

Twice before when we knew that fellow team members had prayed for and were continuing to pray for "Travel Mercies" for us, we wound up missing flights out of England and had to spend a few extra days there. Once, due to traffic and the transfer from Heathrow to Gatwick; and once because we had been reseated on a different plane out of Hong Kong en route from the Philippines due to electrical problems on the plane.

Now, "Electrical Problems" is one of those terms that is used to cover so many things in many different applications: indication of a bad fuse, a faulty connection, a short in the wiring, a bad part—including one of a thousand little capacitor/resistor things on an electrical circuit board which go far beyond my ability to comprehend and fix.

Moreover, I think you would be surprised just how often we use "Electrical Problems" in everyday, commonplace conversation. This may be an indication of our dependence/reliance on electricity and its convenient appliances; or it may be a reminder to us about our "finiteness" and constant search and longing for eternity, perfection, and something that won't break down. Realizing, finally, that it may not be a philosophical problem at all, but could be put down to simply that old Harry forgot to plug the damn thing in and/or that no one ever checked to see if "it" was actually turned on.

Now, in our case, the explanation of "Electrical Problems" didn't really need to come from the pilot. As soon as they unhooked the external power at the terminal, the plane became dark and lost all power. Not really a good sign. I would have myself, with all the confidence of an expert, turned to the passenger sitting next to me and said, "We must be having electrical problems," and would have also mentally patted myself on the back for being so intelligent and wise. (Unfortunately for me, the pilot got there first.)

Well anyway, on our way back from the Philippines heading to Russia, now via Hong Kong, it was happening again.

In the middle of the night, we were reseated and rerouted to Heathrow on the off chance that we could still make our connecting flight back to Russia.

We never did make our flight in time, since we spent four hours being processed and redirected in lines again at Heathrow with an extra hour thrown in for lost baggage. So, once again, we were forced to spend a few extra days in England . . . thanks to Travel Mercies?

(Well, some of you may not think that is really bad or rough, spending extra time in England—not considering, of course, the hour delays, missed flights and waiting in lines when completely exhausted—but if you ever spent any time with those British, you'll quickly realize just how bad that can be. I mean, they don't even speak proper English!) To put a fine point on it, awhile back, I was with my son, who

62

only spoke Russian at the time, standing in the checkout line in a grocery store in Columbus, Ohio. A middle-aged woman in front of us overheard our conversation. The woman smiled at us both, looked at Sasha and said, "Oh, he is so cute, (which he is by the way), does he speak American, too?") I rest my case . . . .

Anyway, since these two travel events happened fairly close to one another in the grand scheme of things, all our friends in Russia began to say things like: "Hey, the next time you're in London, could you pick me up some . . . .", or no matter what our plans were, they would say: "So, you're going through London again?"

It was these events in question that made me begin to wonder and question just what these "Travel Mercies" were/are and whether or not I really wanted them. Apparently too, our missions' director, an MK[6] who lived in Kenya during his early formative years, also had a grandmother who prayed for these "Travel Mercies," and so he, too, was curious as to what these actually were. Intended for our comfort, though perhaps more giving way to the feeling of hesitant anticipation of the unknown, he let us know that, even though he wasn't sure what these "Travel Mercies" were, he was praying for them for us, as well. As I recall, I was a little reluctant in thanking him for this.

Now, perhaps the funny side of this, or hopefully soon to be the funny side of this, is that I am writing this as we are waiting to cross the border from Estonia to Russia. (We had traveled to Estonia to renew our Russian visas.) We have already waited about three hours in a large parking lot outside the city of Narva just for our turn to go through the

---

6 "Missionary kid"

Estonian side of the border. They don't want to crowd the city, so they have the line on the outskirts and send in the cars about five at a time, though not at regular intervals. For instance, we sat initially for almost an hour and not one car moved through. Then five cars went and that was all the movement for about another hour and a half.

Curiosity and impatience having finally gotten the best of me, I went to find out where we stood, at least in the number of things. As it turned out, our number is "147," and I think it is a little early to call it a lucky number. They just waved car number 94 through, so that means we have approximately 52 cars in front of us. *(I also found out that they let certain cars through, outside the line, if they meet certain requirements: traveling with a child of three years or less, senior citizens, some sort of handicapped situation, visas ending within four days, or traveling to go to a funeral.)* Since we couldn't legitimately meet any of those requirements, I began to think of alternative means. I was hesitant, though, to ask the guy in the booth how much it would take to "make an exception in my case" since I didn't know their view of "trying to *'persuade'* an official." I shuddered at the thought of having to wait extra for making such a cultural, not to mention sometimes illegal. faux pas.

I also thought of using the "in case of emergency, use phrase of 'But I'm an American'!?" But, recent events have taken some of the popularity and force from that approach. And actually, of late, that approach can sometimes, for some reasons unknown, be misunderstood—something about the "Arrogant American" stereotype. I am not so sure it really has to do with arrogance more than it has to do with the fact that we just expect everything to work and make sense.

Living in America does not prepare you well for life abroad, long border lines, and oh yes, "Travel Mercies."

Just for a few seconds, I even toyed with the idea of leading a revolt by making a mad dash for the border. It wasn't the wait *per se*, it was more the disorder and lack of information that was getting to me. I couldn't help feeling genuine empathy and real understanding for all those people had finally had it and gone left of center.

You see, this process, since it wasn't spelled out to us (nor were there any signs posted—even ones that we couldn't read), started by driving right up to the border and wondering where was the line and why weren't they letting folks through? *(Author's note: all conversations were in Russian unless otherwise noted).* The one border official was nice, however, and did explain what basically we had to do: drive back out to the "Transervice" area and get a "talonchik" (a small paper slip) that says I paid my 15 Krones (about one dollar or one Euro at this time due to the recent events in the stock market in the States), and then drive back to the border. Seemed simple enough.

Well, we drive up to the Transervice area and walk up to the guard. Here, we are given a *metal token* with a number on it (this case being "147"), which is our number in line just to get the *little paper slip* at another booth, for which we will pay 15 Krones (which was close to a dollar, but by the time I actually will pay for it, the exchange rate may have already changed). And no, I am not being sarcastic . . . .

It is now 2:38 p.m., and we arrived just before 11:00 a.m. to wait for our paper slip and for more cars to be let through the gates to freedom—back to Russia. *(Oh man! You do not know how crazy that actually sounds.)*

Now, this is the good part. After waiting this long and talking to the many others also waiting (most of the travelers knew Russian), including a family from Poland, we figured out the process. When the border guards actually at the border deem it okay, they call the "Transervice" people and say "Send more." The guy in the other booth then sticks his head out of the side window and waves the next five cars through. The whole row of cars then moves up and the next five go and pay their 15 Krones (if that still hasn't changed in the meantime) handing in their metal token/number, receiving their "green talonchik," and waiting until they are waved through by the guy in the booth. And it seemed that this process could take anywhere from one hour to two. Just to give you an example, the guy in front of us was an Estonian, who apparently had done this many times before and lived in Narva. So, he actually left his car at 11:00 a.m., went home and came back around 3 p.m. I don't think I need to say this, but for those who may be wondering, yes, he made it back in time before his turn was up.

(At this time there is a pause in this account, as our row began to show signs of life.)

Believe it or not, sometime around 3:30 p.m., we actually got our little green slip, were waved through and were off to the border.

The remaining part of the border crossing took another hour and a half, so our actual bedlam at the border was a total of six hours. It was a relief to be on the other side and to be moving again. What this meant, at the time, was that our 12 to 13 hour trip just got longer by 6 hours.

Mary took over the driving to get us to St. Petersburg, and then we would switch again as she would navigate, with map in hand as I dealt with the obstacle course and demolition derby of St. Pete traffic, roads and Russian driving. *(Street signs and route signs are considered optional by most Russian Traffic Authorities.)*

Ironically, we had started our trip out intentionally early, leaving from Tallinn so as to miss the evening rush hour in St. Pete. I even pushed it some on the Estonian highway, not stopping, even though I had to go to the bathroom because I wanted to save time by both going to the bathroom and getting food right before the border on the Estonian side at some familiar yellow arches. (Oh, you male drivers would appreciate the sacrifice, pain and concentration it required to just to keep our time low.) You know, "No stopping, don't want to waste time." Well, all of that planning was pretty much shot at the six-hour border crossing. Even the food we had bought, which had been intended for breakfast after we had crossed the border, turned out to be our lunch on the Estonian side. We should have bought enough for dinner, as well.

Well by the time we got to St. Pete, rush hour was pretty much over thanks to our six- hour wait. (Could that be due to Travel Mercies, too?) We stopped by the side of the road to make sandwiches, switch drivers, and begin our race through the city of St. Pete.

Things were, indeed, looking up at this point. And to be honest, that six-hour wait was fading as we were finally making progress toward our goal of home. It struck me, at that moment, that what I used to think of as one of the world's worst nightmares, i.e., getting stuck for endless hours (at that time four or more) at some border crossing, turned out to be livable. (Of course, during that time I wasn't so sure.) Was this lesson a Travel Mercy? Now, I know that people have lived through and are living through more difficult situations and tragedies. This is by no means a comparison to them. It is merely an honest expression of my own vain fears and worries about those things which are beyond my control anyway.

We made fairly good time going through St. Pete, and things were looking even brighter—figuratively speaking. *(You know, where you almost begin singing out loud songs that contain colorful birds on various parts of your body and everything being actually satisfying.)* I was going to switch back and let Mary drive again outside the city, and I let her know that we would do that when we got gas about 100 km from St. Pete. *(You can't waste time by just stopping—need to stop and get gas at the same time—makes perfect sense to most drivers who are goal versus process oriented.)*

This is one of those times where you develop superstitions—especially those of the particular nature of Murphy's Law and all of it corollaries. Like, don't ever say that "things couldn't get worse." In fact, I am not sure you should even allow the thought to cross your mind. Somehow, it seems like somebody out there can hear those thoughts and words spoken into the air and what do you know, it is time for "Travel Mercies" to kick in again.

Lo and behold, we got about 50 km on the other side of St. Pete (now about 9 p.m. local time and still about 375 km left to go on the highway), and I suddenly realized that when I go to down shift our clutch is gone! There was no resistance on the pedal at all. Bad feeling. I don't know if anyone else feels this way when something like that happens, but your mind starts to race and play tricks on you. You start to think maybe I just imagined it or maybe it is not so bad. So, you start pumping furiously on the pedal hoping for some inkling of hydraulic pressure that will allow the clutch to engage.

Well, my feelings went down with the pedal, all the way to the floor. As I am continuing to pump the pedal to no avail, I inform my wife in a very "calm, spiritual" way, perfectly befitting a Christian missionary. *Fortunately for me, some of that communication may be unfit or unsuitable to be published for readers who are young or more sensitive.*

So my wife and I begin this frantic "dialog" about what we should do. I do not want to stop the car, as I am not sure if we could get it going again and thus be truly stuck in the middle of nowhere without a paddle. *(We don't have the same roadside assistance available here, just in case you were wondering.)*

However, at the same time of not wanting to stop the car, I was also looking at the gas tank being half empty. Now this isn't exactly one of those situations that invites conversation or discussion over optimism and pessimism and whether the tank is half-full or half-empty. The truth of the matter was that it would only take us about half of our destination no matter how you looked at it. So here we are, a family of three, late at night on a dark, Russian road with few travelers, potential thieves, and potentially stranded.

Panic was mounting as our options began to fade. What to do? Fortunately, we had our cell phone with us, though we were going in and out of reception areas. Our travel antenna for the phone was misplaced some time ago; and my rigging up of an extra wire was, *unfortunately*, buried under much luggage in the back of the car. The problem still remained. We couldn't exactly stop the car and go in search of it.

So, after a few unsuccessful attempts at calls to friends in our city, and some more "calm" exchanges between my wife and me, she decided to risk climbing to the "way back" of the car and digging to the bottom of the pile of luggage while traveling about 60 mph on a Russian, bumpy-curvy road. By the grace of God, she was successful (without too much bruising) in retrieving the makeshift antenna which gave us some hope of making a phone call. The problem was compounded in that in order to hold the signal, the phone had to be held near the roof of the car. So, you can imagine what ensued next: my wife craning her neck towards the roof of the car, attempting to make a phone call, while the car is swaying and bouncing on the Russian road. *Her expression . . . well, you can only imagine.*

At first, we got through to one of our friends, but they weren't home. We explained the situation briefly to their mom, and she said she would try to pass the information on. However, apparently not fully understanding the problem, she suggested that it would be better if we called back. Without knowing what else to do, we said we would try.

My wife and I got into another small "disagreement" as to what to do next. I impressed upon her that I wanted to at least get hold of our police friend to let him know, and see if he had anything to offer. One thought I had was to try to drive as far as we could, and then have them come out and tow us from there. However, that goal was now being blocked by the fact that we couldn't seem to connect with him, either. His answering machine didn't pick up and our signal went in and out.

As if that weren't enough, the other pressing issue was that we would soon be nearing one of the few gas stations along the way, and we needed to make a decision *soon* as to what we were going to do: stop and get gas, not knowing whether we would be able to move from there, or just drive until we ran out of gas and get as close to home as possible.

There is a funny aside here that, as we later found out from our police friend, three times we actually did connect with his machine, which for some reason that night was set on immediate pick up without an answer. So, as it turned out, several minutes of our ride and conversation were recorded without our awareness. I began to think, "Oh no, what part did they hear?" And "O. S., busted."

Several days later when helping our police friend move some furniture in their new place, I found out just what part of our conversation they heard. Having already confessed to them our rough exchanges, I was amused to discover that amid the noise of the car and static, the only clear, audible words were when we decided to pray, and we spoke loud enough for Sasha to hear in the back seat. Now, how is that for true spirituality?

Well, what happened next was ultimately an answer to prayer; although, at that time, I must admit I didn't think so. (And not only our prayers, I found out later that many of our teammates had started praying when they heard from that mom who wanted us to call back.) Driving from St. Pete to our city, you run through about six small towns where there are police stations, and often the police stand outside and wave cars over to check their documents. Especially late at night, they seem to check all cars going through.

Well, we came upon one of these police stops, and so I

slowed down as per the rules. Now, what goes through my mind is that I could stop and ask for help, but getting going again was still a mystery, and I just wanted to get as far as I could. However, one of the policemen decided differently. He waived us over. So, I pulled over and popped the car out of gear and turned off the engine. The officer introduced himself, very officially, and asked to see my documents. I got out of the car and handed him my documents and began to explain that just recently our clutch had broken *and* that I didn't know what to do. We both took a brief look under the hood, and I tried to add some brake fluid to the clutch line. We both watched it run out underneath the car. The hydraulic line/tube was broken. After discovering where we were headed and how far that was from where we were, he handed back our documents. He went over to confer with one of the other officers regarding what to do with us. He came back and suggested that if we had a good battery and starter, we could start the car in first gear, then shift normally by revving the engine a little and letting off the gas, and then shift smoothly to a higher gear. (I didn't think till later on the road, "what about down shifting?")

Our hopes picked up immensely. We got ourselves settled and buckled in again, looked for a break in the traffic, put the car in first gear, and started her up. She jerked some, and there was a little adjustment as to giving her some gas to keep her going. We moved forward, at first a little rough, until I got the hang of getting her into second. Third came smoothly and so did fourth. We were off and running again towards our Russian home. The remaining challenges that faced us ahead were down now to only five small towns, where you had to slow down going through them. One of those towns had stop lights, and all had police stands where we could be stopped again and have to worry about going again. Oh, yeah, we still needed some gas. And that was only to get us to our city limits within which had a lot of traffic lights, turns, etc.

Having gained some confidence in starting the car, we stopped for gas at about 100 km outside of St. Pete, topped off the tank, and bought some coffee as we figured it would be a late night of travel from there and one of us would need to stay awake for it. Given the circumstances, we felt it best that I drive the rest of the way home. We had one small anxious moment at the gas station, as the car didn't seem to want to start in first, and we had a truck right behind us that wanted us *out of the way*. After a sweaty moment or two, I was finally able to get the car started and moving, once I realized that having the emergency brake on was actually a hindrance to my goal *("brilliant")*. So onward, we went into the night.

We came upon a few challenges of very slow-moving trucks, and since down shifting was not such an easy thing to do, it made passing them all the more necessary—even though at times not legally possible. Three vehicles abreast on a two-lane highway, all of them heading in the same direction. My wife, *(typically a kind, conservative driver)*, tired and exhausted, lifts her head slightly from the back of the seat, glances out the windshield and says, "You can make it," and then closes her eyes and goes back to sleep. One stop light almost brought us to a complete halt, but instead of stopping the car, I veered off onto the shoulder of the road to give us more room. The light changed, and the car ahead of us began to move just in time for me to throw the car into second gear (a little roughly) and keep us moving forward.

By the grace of God *again*, we actually did make it past the five police stands without being hailed, and we did drive all the way through the city to our parking lot and right into our slot at 2:30 a.m. We left all of our stuff in the car and headed up on foot to our flat, thus ending a very long journey filled with "Travel Mercies." Now, it is interesting to note that because it was so late, most of the stop lights in the city were blinking yellow, which allowed us to make it all the way home without stopping. Was this a part of "Travel Mercies?"

Now, in the Bible, fortunately or unfortunately depending upon your perspective, is an occasional verse such as this found in the book of James, "Consider it all joy my brethren when you encounter various trials, for the testing of your faith produces endurance. And let endurance have its perfect result, that you may be perfect (mature) and complete lacking in nothing,"[7] or this one found in the book of Romans, ". . . but we also exult in our tribulations, knowing that tribulation brings about perseverance; and perseverance, proven character; and proven character, hope; and hope does not disappoint, because the love of God has been poured out within our hearts through the Holy Spirit who was given to us."[8]

These are interesting concepts, joy and exultation in tribulation. (And, these were coming from Paul who had had plenty of "Travel Mercies" as we were beginning to

---

7 James 1:2-3, New American Standard Bible®, Copyright © 1960, 1962, 1963, 1968, 1971, 1972, 1973, 1975, 1977, 1995 by The Lockman Foundation.

8 Romans 5:3-5, New American Standard Bible®, Copyright © 1960, 1962, 1963, 1968, 1971, 1972, 1973, 1975, 1977, 1995 by The Lockman Foundation.

understand them.) Now, as I figure it, it is not so much the trials and tribulations themselves that are so joyous, but to what end God can use them in our lives to mature us and build our faith and character. They can also give us a deeper grasp of the hope that we have in God or to show us how He can work and care for us in miraculous ways if we turn to Him. (Apparently, things like maturity and character don't come when things always go right.)

So these "Travel Mercies," while I would like to think and hope that they make all of my journeys smooth and hassle free, I don't believe that to be the case. What I do believe is that these "Travel Mercies" are requests and opportunities to see God at work in difficult situations and trials to help you better appreciate who it is you are really dealing with.

Does then asking for "Travel Mercies" increase your chances of having a rough time of it? Who knows? Perhaps it does.

So, "Travel Mercies": a pathway to character and faith building, an opportunity to know God better, experience Him at work, an adventure in life, and learn joy and exultation in tribulations?—Bring'em on.

Now in all fairness to God, and being thankful for what we do have, we certainly do not know what would have happened had those "Travel Mercies" not been "in effect." One of my fellow teammates commented half jokingly, "Man just imagine if those 'Travel Mercies' weren't there, how bad it could have been."

Your fellow traveler,

P.S. Travel Mercies to you, too.

How to Sell a Car in Russia

Q: How do you sell a car in Russia?

I believe the answer to this puzzling question lies in the answer of some of the best elephant jokes in the history of mankind . . . .

However, to save myself from a lengthy permission process, I am leaving it up to you to research them yourself or recall them from memory, especially the ones referring to the similarities and differences between elephants and certain types of fruit.

So, how do you sell a car in Russia?

Your multiple choice answers: (choose from one of the following)

A. You don't. You hope that someone steals it instead. Though that doesn't free you from the mountains of paperwork, lines and bureaucracies to not pay taxes on a car you no longer have or use.

B. You pay someone to steal it—having given up the hope of someone removing it on their own volition. (Though, that still doesn't free you from the lines and paperwork.)

C. You decide, as one of Pavlov's (or it might have been one of Skinner's) dogs, it is better to take the shock and pain, not sell it and take the loss on the car, pay the annual taxes, and save yourself from the mountain of paperwork, lines and bureaucracy to not pay taxes on a car you no longer own or use. (You have to admit that sounds pretty attractive.)

D. You can't afford to be one of Pavlov's dogs (and you never even heard of Skinner), and so you can't afford the pleasure to be resigned to a glassy-eyed, zombie state with drool hanging out of your mouth, and thus have to commit yourself to selling the car, the mountain of paperwork, lines and bureaucracy to not pay taxes on a car you no longer want.

What you are about read is actual history. Names have been changed to protect those foolish enough to have actually tempted this feat. (Kids do not try this at home—even with adult supervision).

So, I have this friend who lives in Russia . . . who has a birthmark the shape of the Titanic, was prom queen in 1980, and has a wife named Mary and two sons named Alexander and Eugene.

Okay, so I lied about the birthmark. *(It looks more like the boat on which some passengers took an ill-fated, three-hour tour.)*

As for the prom? Heh . . . .

One of the easiest things about this whole story is that I didn't have to work hard to find a buyer. He found me. I merely told the parking lot attendant, where we keep the car, that my wife and I finally decided to sell our old car (our car fund had finally been filled thanks to God and all of our generous supporters). It was a good car, though, while it lasted (a Mitsubishi Space Wagon 1988—sold in Europe, but

77

also sold in America under the name of Colt Vista Wagon). But, it was now costing us more and more to keep running; and we probably wouldn't even get back what we had put into it in the last six months. The short-term projections were not looking that good either as it was getting half the gas mileage it had gotten before, the CV joint was starting to make noise, and the fast-food wrappers were beginning to pile up. If we couldn't have raised the funds for a new car, we would have bitten the bullet, kept it, cleaned it and accepted the ongoing maintenance costs.

As if that weren't enough, the car was built in Germany and *not* designed for Russian roads. If you think they are similar to our own in America, you have no idea just what you are missing. Very few other places can you be assured of never falling asleep at the wheel and spinal compression at the same time. Even when advertising used foreign cars that are imported here for sale, they highlight that "none of the mileage was on Russian roads." "Roads" in Russia is better understood by the observation of one visitor, who, when asked about the presence and condition of Russian roads, replied, "Roads? Didn't see any. But the way was passable." To illustrate the reality of this, I replaced our suspension (shocks and struts) two and a half times in less than five years. Yes, and one of those times was due to our "Travel Mercies" trip when my wife driving failed to execute the necessary "put-the-car-on-two-wheels" maneuver in order to avoid the pothole that blew out the front strut and, at the same time, seemed to remove the space between joint and bone and spinal disks, thus fusing them all together. As in moderate comparison with all my luxury cars in America, (a '77 Chevette, an '83 Pontiac Phoenix, and an '85 Renault

Encore—two of which were hand-me-down "gifts" from my parents), I don't think in all my forty some years in America, I replaced the suspension even once.

Don't let me kid you, cars haven't always been my strong suit . . . . One of my former co-workers even commented once to me, "You know, Macarus, you are not into cars are you?!", as my car did not really fit in with the rest of the newer cars in the parking lot, save for one or two *(and we all knew who those belonged to)*.

Just take my Chevette for example . . . . I remember quite distinctly when my always-very-loving, generous and supportive parents called me while I was in college at OSU (they lived in Downers Grove, Illinois, at the time) and said, "If you don't want the Chevette, we are going to throw it away." What could I say? My first car. Then they informed me it wasn't working. I remember that time very clearly as it was the day of my baptism in a private lake in Ohio. My friend and I had planned later to drive all night with a rented car trailer, grab the Chevette, and return to Ohio. The baptism was very memorable as Mary, too, was baptized at the same time. We, together with several others who had helped us find God, went into the lake, formed a circle, and those of our friends who had already been baptized, baptized us. We left directly following the celebration and headed out for Illinois.

We drove through the night and arrived fairly early in the morning around 4 or 5 a.m. (It is about a seven hour trip for those who do not know the region.) My parents were out of town, so no one was home. I went around back and let myself in, as my parents back then rarely locked the back door. Realizing, that my parents had not left any car keys out, I had a sudden sense of panic. We needed to unlock the steering in order to get the car out of the garage, load it on to the trailer, and have it be free to turn with the trailer.

Fortunately, in my family, we always had "the kitchen (or junk) drawer" which had everything in it you could possibly imagine, save for anything related to the kitchen. In there, I found buried in all of the other junk a spare key or two.

We opened the garage, pushed out the Chevette into the street and then onto the trailer. We thought we were home free. Yet . . . *(and I didn't even know about Travel Mercies at this time).* As we were finishing hooking up the chains, two police cars on silent alarm with flashing lights turned onto our street and headed straight for us.

We looked up, and at each other just briefly, and were somehow frozen with fear. Our hearts were pounding so hard it was difficult to speak. And we knew if we did speak, it would give away our fear, and sound as if we were actually guilty of something. Of course, we both had done our fair share, and perhaps more than our fair share, of running from the police in our youth, which didn't seem at all to help now. ("The guilty flee when no one is pursuing" shortened from "The wicked flee when no one is pursuing, but the righteous are bold as a lion."[9])

You know when you have that sudden fear that all of those things you did wrong and didn't get caught for, or that no one ever knew about, were about to be discovered and you would be led off to jail. And at the same time in your mind, you make that quick deal with God, that if he gets you

9   Proverbs 28:1, New American Standard Bible®, Copyright © 1960, 1962, 1963, 1968, 1971, 1972, 1973, 1975, 1977, 1995 by The Lockman Foundation.

out of this one, you swear you will never do "*that*" again . . . .

The officers exited their cars simultaneously, each with one hand on their pistols and the other holding a flashlight (it was still a little dark).

I believe there are four proven (perhaps only two scientifically), documented, or theorized incidences in science and nature where time actually slows down, or *seems to slow down*.

The first incidence is when your speed (your relative velocity) approaches the speed of light. The closer you get to that limit, the more time slows down. If you should ever happen to reach the speed of light, it is theorized that *time*, for you, would essentially stop. The only problem is that your mass (your absolute bulk—independent of gravity and not to be confused with weight) increases exponentially as you approach the speed of light, and you would eventually become infinitely massive if you ever obtained it. I am not so sure that would be a bad problem to deal with. You would be infinitely massive (*over weight if near or standing on another large massive body*) on the one hand, but you would have all the time in the universe, on the other, in order to lose it. So you could in all likelihood, "get around to it."

The second incidence, I believe, is nearing or being in an intensely high gravitational field. These high "g-fields" are usually found around immensely massive heavenly bodies like in and around black holes. Which means to have time slow down for you, you need to be nearing or residing in a black hole or to just happen to be near your massive friend who just happened to obtain "light speed."

The only problem with this is that very few things, if

81

anything at all, ever leaves a black hole. These black holes are the things in the universe that suck everything into it, including it seems, light itself. So, there is a minor logistical problem there to figure out what to do with your time once you have it.

It would be safe to say that very few people have really experienced that type of black hole personally and written about it.

Now, I know many, including myself, who have at times experienced the third type of what I would call "temporal (or *fugescent*) black holes." Those are the instances where you feel like your whole life is being sucked down into an ethereal blackness, and you are not sure if you are ever going to get out of it. They may happen more frequently to some people and seem at times to be connected with age, major birthdays, puberty, being a teenager, being the parent of a teenager, or being broken in, in love. Time seems to slow down to an almost unbearable pace for people experiencing these types of "holes" in their life. So, while waiting for *Time* to heal all wounds, we find ourselves saying, *"this will never end."*

As an aside, there are two phenomena of black holes not associated with time at all. The first of these are what I would call "random, renegade, floating, small black holes" or "rrfsbh's." These are the explanation to many of the strange disappearances of that second sock (thus eliminating the use of the pair), that one check you had sent out, or the one you were expecting to receive, or that important letter or document that cannot be found. Some people, even without knowing of the existence of these "rrfsbh's" have mistakenly thought that their items merely "vanished in thin air!" We know better now. For a more detailed study of these particular "rrfsbh's," you can read of my investigations, observations, and findings in my book entitled, "Where the Socks Go" by Jonathan L. Macarus, collegiate level. Not *light* reading.

Oh, and for most of you women, this is the explanation for why, when talking to most men, including your husbands, it seems that most, if not all, of the words you've just spoken just disappeared into space, never reaching their intended target.

The second type of time-independent, black hole is more associated with location than anything else. These locative black holes are responsible for the times you might have heard people saying something like, "he got off the plane, and fell into a black hole." "It's like she fell off the planet" (when in reality she really fell into one of these types of black holes) or, "going to that place is like going into a black hole." One or several aspects of locative, temporal and regular black holes can be in operation here; that of sucking the remainder of whatever life you have left in you out of you. And/or nothing or no one ever seems to come out of there (or at least not the same way as they went in). I have to confess that Russia, at times, feels like it approaches this definition.

The final and fourth incidence of time slowing down (not associated with black holes) seems to be when your heart is pumping so hard it is all that you hear, that and your heavy breathing. These incidences are mostly found or experienced in high-fear adrenaline situations where it seems your heart is pumping your blood close to the speed of light. (Some have extrapolated this to include the incidences of great anticipation of something good or awesome, as well. However, I believe it is the back of the mind suspicion, doubt, and fear of actually "not getting that which was anticipated" which in turn creates the high-fear adrenaline situation. See "Where The Socks Go," pp. 2343-3241.)

It was this fourth type, my friend and I were experiencing as we were standing in front of the police . . . .

Needless to say, we moved really slowly and were trembling (hopefully only on the inside) with fear. The policemen asked for our identification, and then asked us what *we were doing* at such an early hour with the car and trailer.

It began to dawn on me that one of my neighbors must have called the police thinking we were stealing a car. As we nervously handed over our identification, the police then confirmed the obvious that that is what they suspected of us. Then another thought hit me and my youthful cockiness (of which I have since outgrown . . . except for the cockiness), and I couldn't contain myself. I looked at both officers and said, "Right. Two guys rented a trailer to drive all the way from Ohio, just to steal a '77 Chevette, *that wasn't even working?!?"*

The younger of the two seemed to smile in agreement. The older one apparently had no sense of humor. He gripped his pistol more tightly and waited as the younger officer examined our identification. (Perhaps it was just that my timing and delivery were off?) Fortunately for us, I still had my old Illinois (no, you do not pronounce the "s") drivers license that had my folks' address listed as my residence. The demeanor of both officers seemed to soften as they too reflected on the humorousness/ridiculousness of the whole situation. They handed back our identification and started for their cars. Just then, the younger stopped and ran back and asked for my license again to write the information down just in case we were actually stealing a vintage, non-mint condition—with replaced floor boards by my father with two-by-fours and sheet metal—non-running '77 Chevette *that* I learned later would require changing the starter and solenoid just about as often as the oil (so often that I began to carry a spare one in the car).

We left as quickly as we could, still shaken from the experience. My friend just wanted to get out of town before something else happened. I never did sell that car. I "gave" it to a friend in our home church with the warning of "don't take it on the highway, or else . . . ." Within a week and a half, I found out he had the car up on blocks in his front yard. Apparently, he had taken it on the highway. In this case, the *"or else"* meant blowing a rod and shooting a piston right through the engine.

————

Now back in Russia, present day.

Two and a half days of waiting, standing in lines, running around, inspections, documents, and two burned fingers (fortunately, only one of them mine), plus an additional five minutes, were required to sell our old car in Russia.

"You have absolutely no idea," would be a good beginning . . . .

Tuesday, 10:30 a.m., somewhere in a small city in Russia . . . . heading for a bank.

In order to sell a car in Russia, you first have to remove it from the "department" of records. This puts the car in kind

85

of a limbo or transitional state, where it is viewed as "in transit," which means still in your ownership, but not in full use, and intended for sale or return to your full use later. (Please accept the wordage and verbiage as an artistic style to draw the reader in to a fuller understanding and taste of the red tape, blue tape and all of the other color tapes associated with the actual procedure here.)

In order to actually begin this process, what is needed is to pay two fees at the bank. One for "transit tags" and the other is for the actual process of removal from the records. I know it sounds easy so far . . . . However, paying bills in Russia isn't quite up to our automatic bill payment withdrawal system back in the States.

Instead of sending you bills that have all of the needed information on them, many of the government fees are paid using blank forms where you fill in all of the numbers and information yourself. Each one of these blanks requires four or five strings of account or identification numbers, one of which contains 20 digits. And, as if that weren't sufficiently challenging, the space for the largest number just happens to be the smallest on the form. (And no, I am not kidding.) So, in all, a total of 66 digits. However, each blank has a duplicate lower half that requires the exact same information to be filled out, as well. So, that is 132 digits per blank on one side, not including the date. So, if you include the date, that is an additional six digits per half (if for the sake of economizing time, you only use two digits for the year instead of four). This makes a total of 144 digits per blank plus all of the other needed information.

Since I had two fees to pay, that meant two blanks with different information and a different number or two, and thus brought the total up to 288 digits. Because I really was trying to save time by not standing in another line on another day, I also brought along information to pay another bill, so that made it an additional 144 digits bringing the morning's total to 432 digits to write to pay for a combined total of three dollars and twenty five cents ($3.25).

Tuesday, 11:30 a.m. Still in that same, small city in Russia . . . . leaving bank, heading for car.

Now, in order to actually remove the car from the records, the vehicle identification number and the engine identification number need to be checked against the original documents at an official technical inspection facility. The vehicle and these numbers have to be clean in order for them to even look at your car.

I drove over to one of the inspection stations and saw that the line was fairly long, so I drove across town to the only other one I knew about. The line there was only about 11 cars, which meant that the wait would probably be an hour or so. It turned out to be lunchtime, so the place was on break anyway and wouldn't start taking cars in for another 15 minutes. (Hence, the small line in the first place).

Tuesday, 12:45 p.m.

Once the facility opened again, I went in another door and stood in line for another form to show my documents and ask my ubiquitous and important question of, "just what is needed from me in order to do this?" The oddly amusing thing to most of the officials I met that day was that of "What on earth is an American doing trying to take off record a Russian-registered vehicle?" By that time, I was beginning to wonder the same thing myself. (You see the car wasn't purchased in our names as it was easier and safer to have a

Russian buy it for us and be acting as the owner. We were operating the car under an official agreement and with an official permission slip.) I filled out the form in the car, went back in to the window and got the official stamp put on the form in the place where the inspector would check off the numbers for comparison to the documents.

Tuesday, time—it was beginning not to matter anymore.

I finally made it into the inspection area and tried to wipe off the "VIN" to make it more visible. I couldn't remember where the engine number was, only that it was not easy to find when I had initially bought the car and had to do this same process in reverse which was several years ago. Back then, the original documents initially listed the engine number as being absent. However, the one young, aspiring inspection officer who looked my car over, decided not to give up that easily. He eventually did find it. Unfortunately, it was rusty and corroded. Therefore, he sent me to find a mechanic who could actually reach the number to clean it with some light sandpaper and to use some chalk on it to make it more readable. We did just that, and I drove back to the inspector. Only to be sent back to try again. Finally, the third time with the inspector was sufficient, and I made it through the actual purchase process of the car. It did, however, require some additional paperwork and official stamps, as the engine number had to be added to the documents.

––––––

Now, some five years later, that diligence, youthful, full-of-hope-for-change of that first inspector was coming back to haunt me.

I, personally, do not know of any country that utilizes the

engine number as part of their official registration and process. It might be that in Russia, you can buy complete frames apart from the engine (since they do not last too long with rust, etc.) or because you want to keep track of everything to confirm whether it is original or not. Or it might be that car theft, being so prevalent, people began stealing engines as a far more lucrative and sneaky business. Of course, it could be as simple as, "the system that was begun a long time ago of registering both the horse and carriage has continued to this day, and no one really now knows why." Or lastly, it has to do with matters of Life and Time . . . .

For the purposes of illustrating this last principle, a simplified equation of life can be found below.
Life = the sum of the following:

$$(Exp+RIG+MPS+mps+Lr+Wp-T/t) \times (Li).$$

This equation is translated thus:

●Exp=Experience—can be positive or negative depending upon Perspective and can be significantly affected by our RIG.

●RIG=Relationship and Influence of God—the existence of a Personal Relationship with God (i.e. you are actually in His family, considered one of His children via adoption through Christ), and His Influence in your life.

●MPS = Meaning & Purpose & Significance—eternal (pursuits/goals of people: love and care of others, helping others find God, forgiveness and eternal life—all things that in the end, are really important and can last forever).

●mps = meaning & purpose & significance—temporal (pursuits/goals of things like: money, wealth, comfort, achievement [an Olympic gold medal, etc.], success, knowledge, accomplishment—all things that, perhaps even though not bad or even some good, in the end, will pass away).

- Lr = Love received.
- W = Work.
- T = Time of Work of Public Officials—their time at work which is a finite number and typically the difference somewhere between 9 a.m. and 5 p.m.
- T = your time
- p = pay—which is nearly constant and usually, except for those in high public representative positions, practically insignificant
- Li = Love—imparted to others; one of, if not the most significant variables of our experience of life. The greater we love others, the direct multiple increase in our Life sum.

Without waxing too philosophical at this point, here is what I mean. Our lives are the summation of the interconnected and independent variables as listed above and again below for easy reference.

Life=sum of the following:

$$(Exp+RIG+MPS+mps+Lr+Wp-T/t) \times (Li).$$

As with most complex equations that scientists really cannot solve or know all of the variables and constants, we start to make assumptions that seem reasonable (or at least to us) in order to simplify the equation. We do this in order to put some numbers down so that we can actually get some numbers out, so that in the end we can be tested on it at the university level. (Some, though, have taken this further and used it to subsequently rate performance and ability to live our lives and solve complex equations.) But in reality, what is tested is just our ability to remember the basic life equation and those basic assumptions and how well we can cheat and get away with it. As with complex equations, the more assumptions one makes, the easier the equation and life become.

Strange as it may sound, the reverse is also true, however; and as often happens in the fuss and worry of life, we can make life more confusing and complex than, in reality, it is by even adding imaginary variables to the life equation. Unfortunately, it sometimes takes the death of a loved one for us to get back to the most important and real variables. (The only anomaly in all of nature seems to be that governments and tax laws work purposefully and are governed mysteriously towards more complexity, trying to find the ideal or perfect match of "totally complex and perfectly confusing" in order to make everyone else's life more difficult to figure out.)

Back to the equation: so, if we look at the equation through the eyes of a person just going through life who has not found God yet and thus the eternal MPSs, this is what life is reduced to:

$$L=(Exp+mps+Lr+Wp-T/t) \times (Li).$$

With further assumptions like: we become tired and worn down by the world, so that our Exp becomes something to be endured instead of an adventure. And so we become only interested in our Exp from an entertainment point of view, hopping from one source of entertainment to another in search of lasting of joy and fulfillment. Therefore, Experience becomes identified with entertainment; hence, our Exp as a value drops to 0.

Our mps, being temporal, don't really satisfy us in the long run, and those things which we thought would make us happy and fulfilled continue to change since we realize we didn't achieve it with the last thing we held to be so important. It, too, drops in value.

Love received is nice and great, but it is not something you can control. Nor in a world where everyone seems to be looking out for themselves more and more, is it something you can really rely on. Hence this too drops.

Since you are not receiving a great deal of love, and are not experiencing the infinite love of God yet, you are hardly feeling up to the part of loving others let alone getting up off the couch to change the channel (thank God for remotes), which means your Li (Love Imparted) drops significantly and thus, your overall Life sum.

So what are we really left with? For most it may have been in the back of your mind all along thinking this is what life is all about.

$$L = Wp - T/t$$

Life = Work x pay - time of public officials/your time

And since your time is not viewed as that valuable by public officials, it can go to infinity, thus reducing the felt effect of their fixed time at work. So, life becomes just the result of:

$$\text{Work} \times \text{pay} \ (\text{Life} = \text{Work} \times \text{pay})$$

or in essence "Life is work;" thus explaining that common experience of when work sucks, your life seems to as well.

It may also explain why people can get so wrapped up in work, lose themselves in their work, or take their identity from their work, because that is what Life has become.

Following this further . . . work, much like the fixed constant of the speed of light, seems to be an unchanging constant demand on life, so the only really felt, changeable influence on life becomes your pay. Which is why, then, so many people focus on and complain about it as if it were the only important thing in life? How interesting . . . .

So where does that leave us? Public officials bitter at life, hating their work and complaining about their pay are not moved in any way to reduce your time and thus increase their felt effect of their fixed time at work. So you are stuck.

Still Tuesday.

Well, as my luck would have it now, in the present wanting to sell the car, the inspector could not even find the number on the engine. I tried to give him the general ballpark of where I remembered it to be, but it didn't help. After about ten minutes, he gave up and wrote something down on the paper and sent me to the central headquarters of this particular police division (not in this facility but, fortunately not too, far), third floor, 15th cabinet.

So off I drove . . . to another line . . . .

I found the office and went in. They told me to wait out

93

in the hall. They didn't really tell me what I was waiting for. During that time, as I stood by, another Russian came up and went right in. He didn't come back out. So, I poked my head in again and saw that he was now getting his own matters dealt with. Great. I went back out in the hall and stood right by the door with my "none shall pass" look. (It wouldn't be until later I would realize just how much more time the maneuver that guy pulled would cost me.) Once that guy left, I headed in. I handed my documents to the inspector/officer and explained the situation to him. He told me to wait outside in the courtyard of the building.

So off I went. The other guy who went in front of me was also there. We waited for about an hour until the officer came out. We thought he would just take a look himself, but we wound up driving to the other technical inspection station (the one that had the huge line earlier in the day) and went into the garage from the back side. So, at least I was able to skip another line . . . or so I thought. Well, the guy who ducked in front of me happened to be in the process of buying a brand new fancy Honda. His problem, too, was that they couldn't find the engine number. Well, instead of putting a few people on his car and sending someone to my car, they all hovered around his car—they were very impressed by his purchase—for well over an hour. It even got to the point where they asked to borrow a wrench from me so that they could remove one of the covers on his engine just in case the number would be more visible. I was only too willing to try to help expedite matters.

When after an hour or so and they still hadn't found the number on his car, finally, two inspectors came down to look at my car. Fortunately, it didn't take them long to find the number. Unfortunately, it was now even more rusted and corroded and completely unreadable. They directed me to where I could see it and reach it if I used long-reaching contortionist techniques, *AND* they instructed me *AGAIN* to try to clean it. So, I spent the next 15 minutes trying to wipe it off using whatever cleaning fluid I could find in my car, but to no avail. They told me I would have to try to clean it off using some rust remover and come back tomorrow. "Wonderful, jusssttt wonderful."

Now, as if that wasn't enough salt in the wound, they then asked me if I could give them a ride back to their office. Now, there was an opportunity for me to explain God's loving grace and forgiveness!?!

I dropped them off, headed towards home and on my way stopped off at the auto parts store to pick up some rust remover.

I arrived home at 5:20 p.m., having no lunch and having accomplished practically nothing for the entire day.

It turned out, too, that my wife had not had a particularly great day with the kids either. But by God's grace, she had compassion and understanding and did not require that I immediately wrestle the kids into submission. She knew, as well as I did, that given my current state, it would have been a battle I might have lost. I sat down on the kitchen floor explaining things to my wife, and simultaneously laughed and cried from holding in all of the frustration and emotion all day and in dealing with this "system" here. I told her that today, I felt like the system was winning, and that I was nearing the point of saying "uncle." The only problem was that also required more energy than I had at the moment.

Wednesday, 2:00 p.m. (Earlier that day, the men on our

team gathered for prayer. And no, it wasn't due to the car. That was our normally scheduled prayer time. Though at the end, I must confess, I did toss up a selfish request for God's help in making my car disappear)

After that, I went down to the car to try to clean off the engine number. A second minor complication was that I wasn't really sure just how I was going to know if I was doing any good or not. I couldn't see the number even if it was clean. However, using tricks that any TV hero making a bomb out of a chocolate bar would be proud of, I fashioned an extension mirror out of one of my wife's compact mirrors (without her consent—a risk, at this point, I was willing to take), a used chopstick, and some duct tape. Then, I went and tried to liberally apply the rust remover to the engine-number area. After several applications and much straining, etc., I tried to examine my work. Unfortunately, it seemed as if I was making it worse and removing what numbers there were.

I then decided to try to drive around and see if I couldn't find something like "Naval Jelly" (not for cleaning belly buttons), since the stuff I had found was very thin, like water. It turned out that in one section of town I might just find it. So, off I went again. Unfortunately, they didn't have it there either. What I did find was one kiosk worker who just recently used the stuff I was working with. She explained how to use it more efficiently and then rinse the area with water.

With a renewed sense of hope, I ran back to the car, grabbed the bottle of rust remover, and in my haste, waved off the gloves, forgetting that the engine would now be very hot after running around town. *Hence the burned finger.*

Realizing my foolish mistake and uttering some "spiritually reflective" words like "Jesus, that hurts" and "God Almighty," I drove home, nursing my finger.

I put the car in the lot as it was getting dark and decided to try again in the morning before going to police division again. Time now: Wednesday, sometime after 7 p.m.

Thursday, 9 something a.m.

I again attempted more cleaning of the engine number. This time I also took some of my wife's kitchen cleanser bought here in Russia supposedly good for removing rust stains. I did a combination of both the rust remover and cleanser, and I still wasn't convinced I was making things better instead of worse. I called the prospective buyer and filled him in on the situation, and he expressed his willingness to meet me at the police division and work on the problem together.

Off I drove . . . *again*.

We met at the building, and he went in to see if one of the inspectors was going to come out. Instead, they sent us back out to the technical inspection station to go through again. (Apparently, they forgot about the ride I gave them and that indeed they said I could just come back to them.) Once again, having to wait in line to go through the inspection facility, the buyer, feeling a sense of hope and desiring accomplishment, wanted to try his own hand at cleaning the number. I explained what I had already done; and he, from the advice of others, seemed to think that all it would take is a few applications of this rust treatment stuff and all would be like new. I also tried to explain the difficulty of trying to clean the number with the engine being hot and to warn him off of it, but apparently my words must have slipped into one of those "rrfsbh's" as they apparently never reached their intended target. History repeated itself and thus, the second burned finger. (As a matter of fact, the same exact finger that I had burned, too.)

By the time our turn came up, we weren't sure what the inspector would find.

But to our surprise, he said he actually saw the numbers and, therefore, signed off on the needed form. The buyer pleaded with the inspector if he wouldn't also sign off on a new identical form that would be required from him when he came back after purchasing the car (just in case there were future problems or questions with the number). Now, to the unwary reader, that point might have been missed. The fact that I, trying to sell my car, have to remove it from the registry by getting the numbers read and signed off by an inspector. And then, the buyer, needing to get the car put on the records, has to do the exact same thing. So, it is quite possible, if you do not experience problems in reading the engine numbers and no other form of black holes, your car could actually pass through the same paperwork and inspection (even inspector) twice in the same day. Doesn't that seem to you as a bit foolish and a little bit inefficient? Not here. Not where they recognize not only the possibility, but the actual existence of, "locational black holes" that can occur while a car is in that limbo "in transit" state.

Thursday, around noon.

We drove from the tech station back to the police division headquarters where I was to turn in that document, my old plates, and my two receipts from Tuesday morning. There was a line (surprise, surprise). The receiving windows close from noon to 1:00 p.m. for lunch. So, it was clear we weren't going to make it before lunch. Fortunately, the buyer went up to the side of the window just to make sure what was going to be needed since I was actually selling the car via a POA (power of attorney) notarized document. It was a good thing he did. As The Fate would have it, there was a new law just recently passed requiring that a *notarized copy* of the notarized POA also be submitted to complete the process.

That left us heading back downtown in search of a notary. The first one we came to was just leaving for lunch. She was nice enough to direct us to another down the street that generally took lunch a half an hour later. Off we went again.

No line. Things were actually looking up.

We drove back and got back in line at the window before their lunch break was over. There were about four or five guys in front of us. That stretch, apart from the general waiting time, seemed to go fairly smoothly, though there was some question about the document and the engine numbers again. We did our best "oh, sure" and "everything was checked out by the inspectors" and so the guy finally received the documents.

Again, to our relief, the guy said our transit documents and tags would be ready by 5:00 p.m. This meant there was still hope to actually sell the car that day and transfer everything to the new owner. (I am not so sure why he wanted it so badly, but he would soon find out that wanting is not the same as having. And, that if he should ever have it, getting rid of it was a real pain in the back side.)

So, we drove to the buyer's apartment where he kept the money for the purchase of the car. I told him that, if possible, I would like to have the money checked to make sure it wasn't counterfeit. Here, in Russia, there is a *real* problem with fake U. S. dollars and some Russian high-note rubles, not to mention that my police friend even recommended making sure about it.

We collected his money and headed for the bank where they exchange money and have the special light needed to make sure of the origin. One of the most ironic sights, though, is that near many of these official money exchanges and banks is the presence of another money-changing agent standing nearby or in a car. Hence, the term "bank on wheels" here. These folks operate their own money exchange operation, and it is not totally clear for whom they actually work. One thing that is clear is that although it is "illegal," these guys are there all the time even in the presence of the police. Something is out of place or rotten in some Scandinavian country. (I've also witnessed these "bank on wheels" people going to the back door of the bank they are next to and exchange cash.)

On the positive side of things, these guys are there when the banks are closed or have run out of rubles and you need to change some money to fulfill other obligations. (Not that I am admitting anything here, or at least nothing that would stand up in court.) The other positive aspect is that these guys are definitely the experts in spotting phony money. They handle the real stuff all the time, and their wellbeing is determined by their ability to distinguish the real from the fake. Basically, if these guys are wrong and trade bad money, they are out of a job, and perhaps a little more than that.

So, it turned out in this case, to economize on time and reduce the number of lines, we chose to utilize the "drive-up window" to check over the money. It was neat to watch as the man quickly handled the money, felt it and held it up both perpendicular and at an angle to the light and checked it over for us, to both of our satisfaction.

So, in less than ten minutes we were leaving the "bank," and heading for our team garage to get the winter tires that went along with the car purchase. We tended to a few other items, and then headed back to the police division to see, if by chance, they might have finished the transit documents a little early.

Thursday, 4:30pm.

Arrived back at police division headquarters and went up to the window. Fortuitously for us, there was only one person in line ahead of us.

When it was our turn, we asked politely, knowing that it was early but just in case, if by chance our documents were ready, as the window on the second floor where you can actually buy or sell a car was only open to 5:30 p.m. The guy at the window was the same guy who had taken our documents. He was in a fairly good mood (probably as it was nearing the end of his day and public service time), so he asked some of the other women there who actually do the processing of documents, if ours were ready. We could hear their response. "Oh, you mean that American?" followed by the laughter of all of the other women and a smile by the guy who had taken our documents. Apparently, there weren't too many Americans who had lost their way and wound up at their window trying to take a car off the registry in Russia. And the thought of it was just as absurd to them as it was to me. I made some comment to that effect, and they all laughed again. Bingo. One of the women still chuckling said that she already had processed our documents and that they were, indeed, ready.

I thanked them from the bottom of my heart, and off we went to actually try to sell the car at another window on the floor below.

Thursday, 5:00 p.m.

No line at the window. However, the women behind the counter were drinking tea and having some kind of sweets with it, so they weren't all too eager to hop up and help us. However, they directed us over to the neighboring window (still no line) where there was a woman who would.

Thursday, 5:05 p.m.

We were all done. The documents signed and filled out, the money transferred. Our car was actually sold. I couldn't believe it. The actual selling and buying of the car took only five minutes. All the other time was just to get it in the limbo or transitional state in order to be able to sell it. Whew . . . unbelievable! I felt like celebrating. The Russians tend to celebrate (with drinking) purchases ranging from minor things like TVs, fridges, etc, all the way up to cars and apartments (as if they needed one more reason for a drinking party). They call it "washing." Of course, the traditional "rinse water" is vodka, and it is for internal use only.

I wanted to institute a new tradition, starting immediately, with the sale of my car.
It felt really good.

So, in closing I will leave you with a few remarks and wisdom from that same book of long ago by referring again to those elephant jokes. Only this time, these are the ones that talk about how to dispatch particularly colored elephants with the appropriate, right-colored weapon. It is a little

unfortunate as the riddle and solution to these particular jokes sound sooooo Russian.
With warm regards,
Jon

The Technical Inspection

To my chagrin . . . *(Does anybody really use that in day-to-day conversation, and actually know what he or she is talking about?)* . . . .

Needless to say, it has been a long time since I wrote last. The whole selling-the-car bit took a lot out of me.

This time, it actually took three events combined to overcome the inertia and threshold for the thoughts to actually come out onto paper and to overcome the exhaustion of dealing with two growing boys of 5 and 11. And did I mention I live in Russia?

Now back to the beginning . . . .

Come to think about it, why do people when they write mystery novels or maybe even romance ones *(I can only assume here)* use language that is never used in common everyday communication nor, would I conjecture (*conjecture* —"hazard a guess but much more intellectually sounding"), in our thoughts to ourselves? I mean, how often have you looked at someone and actually thought, "How *sardonic* his face looks?"

Or, in looking at my surroundings in Russia, how many times have I thought to myself: "the trash is *ubiquitous*?" Or, when looking at that cute, little puppy or some girl's young boyfriend, think "My, how *obsequious* he is." I mean come on. Really, now!?!

Now, not growing up in Massachusetts (where you never end your sentences with prepositions or perhaps even propositions), nor among the upper crust in the States or in Great Britain, it never even dawns on me to have a more "sophisticated" mental conversation *with myself*, nor out loud with anyone else, that has any more meaning and impact on someone's heart and mind than merely to say that "it", actually referring to the trash in Russia, is everywhere.

And, besides, in what other context have you read, heard or said to yourself, "*turgid*"?

In apparent fact, the only time these are used in everyday language is when you are talking about what these words actually mean, having just come across them in these types of books. *(That is if you are honest enough to admit: 1) that you just read these in some romance novel or hopefully a mystery detective one, and 2) that you don't know what they in fact really mean.)* Oh, I suppose there is the third possibility of these words having found themselves embedded, just for "funzies," in a crossword puzzle or two. But, anyone who would offer that excuse is like the person who says they buy girly magazines just for the interesting articles . . . .

These types of words are used by writers who are trying to step out of their boundaries of vocabulary, trying to prove themselves as more educated than the average reader. As if using these words alone gave rise or title to artistic talent, mastery and creativity. When we know it is really the handling of the sword that makes the swordsman. Any man, woman or child can own a dictionary or a fantastic, expensive blade, but it is not in the ownership that determines the skill of the person. It is the poor orphan, who using the most meager and humblest of weapons, grows up to be a master skilled in the art and a defender of those less fortunate using nothing more than a wooden spoon.

For example, take the action, mild, *by today's standards*, violent adventure movie, where our hero kills one of his opponents with a mere teacup made of tin. Now that is priceless, and to say nothing of the acting . . . . Thus, illustrating the point, who needs a rigid, stiff, erect, unbending (at this present time) tea cup, when merely a hard one will do?

And to put a fine point on it, not one of those *four questionable words* mentioned above are even found in many early Basic English dictionaries. Now this leads the reader to one of two possible conclusions. One, the writers of those dictionaries did not know the meaning of those words and thus overlooked them in the compiling of their dictionaries. Or, two, that given the suspected spinsterhood of these early dictionary writers, or their likely roots in a conservative Christian, southern upbringing, they probably never read any romance novels, *and,* for whom merely the thought of the word "*turgid*" had to be connected with the other word also of "*sinful-evil-wicked-worldly and just downright naughty.*"

As for the real reasons for writing—that is, my own here, I am getting to that . . . .

Two of the three reasons have to do with the ridiculous notion of trying to keep a car in Russia. And, now I am sure you're wondering what the third reason could possibly be. Good for you.

Every year, your car, if you happen to live in Russia, has

to undergo and pass a police technical inspection. Now perhaps at the outset that doesn't seem so bad . . . .

If you remember from one of my previous adventures of actually trying to sell a car in Russia, one of the first things you need to do is start at the bank with one of those forms where you can spend about a half an hour copying about 166 digits to pay in advance for the inspection. By God's grace, modern technology, and capitalism put to use, within the last year or so, you can now pay 10 rubles to have the bank clerk print one out for you with all the numbers on it. Some of the best 35 cents I ever spent.

Now, we'll move on to the tricky part. To actually legally pass your technical inspection, your car actually should/needs to be in good working order and recently washed. No small feat for driving on Russian roads. And to top it off, the inspection stations are *replete* (*replete*—"lots, full of") with all fairly modern German equipment. So you have German specifications and precision instrumentation used for testing Russian and foreign made cars that are driven (nearly shaken to death) on Russian roads. *For three years in a row, I have had to replace the ball joints and tie rod ends, and over the past five years, half as many suspension systems of shocks and struts, and one set of leaf springs.*

Now in years past, let's just say, hypothetically, that I had this friend who used to go with another not-so-hypothetical friend who knew someone who made this whole process very easy. Back then, it is rumored, that his car didn't even have to come along for the ride. In reality, my guess is that less than half of the cars on the Russian roads would actually pass the real technical inspection. The other more than half probably have one of those hypothetical friends and don't show up for their annual physical.

Just for added color, during one of our old Bible studies, one of the former policemen shared how he had stopped a car that shouldn't have been on the road. He started reading the riot act to the fellow who owned it for it was in absolutely no condition to be seen anywhere except leaving a demolition derby. He wanted to know who on earth would approve such a car. He looked at the inspection card and much to his *"chagrin" (you know, another word for disappointment and/ or let down of a surprise—hey, even most Basic English dictionaries approve of this word)*, saw that *he was the one* who had signed off on it. What could you do? Apparently in this hypothetical case, the friend who had approached him had lied about his friend's car condition. When in Russia . . . or perhaps, only in Russia?

And, we are only getting warmed up. You can even buy (for only 10 rubles—another 35 cents well spent) in the kiosks on the street laminated calendars that are the identical size as the technical inspection cards, and on the other side of the calendar is an identical imitation technical inspection card with the right year on it. Without a closer examination of this card in your windshield, it would not be possible for a particular pedestrian in uniform to know whether someone was "driving on a calendar" or *not*. Even one of my ex-police buddies told me at one time that even he was riding on a calendar due to the condition of his car.

In returning to my original, hypothetical friend from before, he also, in between inspections (meaning the car was running but needed certain repairs to pass the exam), may have for a short period of time rode under a calendar as well.

(Now, for those technically detailed persons, short is a relative term. What is short to some, may seem like a month or two to others.)

Now, though, with new, stricter laws and rulings from the government that "require" all cars to actually go through and pass the inspection, the looking forward to this event has even more trepidation *(fear, that is)* associated with it. What this means, in reality, is that there is now an increase in the unofficial cost if you want to avoid the Christmas rush and all those nasty lines with pushing and shoving.

To top it off, there were several hurdles to passing the inspection this year. My hypothetical friend's car had an electrical problem and the high beams would only come on and stay on if you held the switch down manually. The other problem was that to take a car through the inspection, the driver has to pass a Russian medical inspection and have in his possession a legitimate certificate to that account. Now we are arriving at the second point . . . and we are just getting started.

To get this medical certificate, one must not only be healthy, but a person of character, extremely talented and assertive. One, who has not been born into this culture, could never accomplish it without outside help. Once you are fortunate to find out *where* (the two or three places) in the city that you can actually obtain this and *when*, you are then amassing the resolve to go and do it.

You have to pass through four doctors' stations in one hour, and you are competing with all of the other drivers, current and aspiring, who are trying to do the same. The challenge is that there isn't any real order to the system, as one, from say a more-developed country, might expect. You do not simply take a number and wait your turn for the entry into the stations, as you might think to be a good idea, and then to be passed on to the following stations in that same order and fashion. No, that would make too much sense, give the people some sense of hope and control, and reduce the *in vivo* test of character. Rather, here in Russia, you would have people first, stand in line at the head-doctor/registry station just to get the "approved" blank form on which they glue your picture to it and then, get it back with four cabinet/room numbers written on it.

Your mission, if you choose to accept it, is to simultaneously stand in four lines, not with numbers or anything as simple as that, but by asking the crowd in the corridor huddled around one particular room, "who is last?" And, then giving the appropriate nod, finger pointing and statement, "I am behind you" to officially hold the claim. You have secured your position, but it is not over yet. You then have to stay on guard and protect your claim to any who comes after you and asks, "who is last?" and either indicate yourself or those who came after you.

You also have to be aware that people will come up just as you are about the next person in line to go through the door, and they will say, "I was behind so and so" indicating the person who had just gone in. So, you wait patiently, praying that you will make it all in time and for a little more patience to not get angry and punch those with whom you came to share about the love of God.

One thing you should know, *Jim*, the lines though do not move at the same pace. So it is possible for you to actually be fourth in line for one and first in line for another. If you miss your turn, you're in trouble.

If it will help in furthering your understanding, I will now relate *my own* experiences in the matter.

I would have been totally lost if it had not been for a good friend of mine (ex-police officer now turned security guard) who was willing to sacrifice a lot of his time with me, and help me run with the bulls and run interference with me. He even got a kick out of trying the "He's an American" in order to see if that wouldn't get me to the front of the line. Don't laugh. He talked so fast, he left one poor guy standing there with a puzzled look on his face, as my friend pushed me through the door to the psychiatrist. (Not even one of the four stations as it turned out—there were two more that I will come to later.) He got me through the registry and into the first of the lines. After a bit, he went and "occupied" "my" place in two of the other lines.

If it is possible to describe in words, both "frenetic" and "agonizingly slow at times" would come close. There were moments it seemed like the wait in the hall was not going to end, and we wouldn't make it before they close. Then, very abruptly, there would be movement, and I would finally make it to the door for which I had been waiting so long just to see one of the doctors. You can become very excited and thankful for the little things in Russia . . . . Not yet, though, to the wetting of my pants, but just give me a few more years here . . . .

And if it weren't for the "gumption" *(aw, to heck with the Basic English dictionaries)* of my Russian friend who wasn't afraid to enter into the fray, I would have never have gotten through it in time. Now, so far, this doesn't even cover the actual doctors' examinations themselves.

The first was eyes and ears. As I came in the door, this

fairly large woman sitting at her desk started in immediately at me for why I was carrying my black bag for documents. She asked me, "where was I getting ready to go to with that in my hand?" I didn't know what to say, *and* I didn't even know I was committing a felony. She then told me to sit next to her on the stool. I thought the stool was a little too close to her *(and you would have also)*, so I drew it away slightly. Mistake number two. Mistake number one was approaching her, in the first place, without my guard up, prior to establishing whether or not the alien was friendly.

So, now she is yelling at me again, firing questions at me, and I felt like I was in school again. After I finally convinced her that I had no idea what the *proper* order of things was since I had never gone through this before *and* that I didn't have an ear problem, but my understanding of the Russian language, especially the medical terms used for things like motion sickness and vertigo, was not great, she finally softened. She did pass me, but when she looked at my written eyeglass prescription from the States (they use a totally different numbering system here by the way), she marked off that I could only drive a personal car and not a public transport vehicle like a trolley bus or a route taxi-minivan. Not that those had occurred to me anyway, but the feeling of rejection was none-the-less felt. *It's not like I was trying out to be a fighter pilot or something.* I found out later, too, that these restrictions still apply to many things, including being a police officer. Old laws and restrictions don't die easily, though there may be a change in the name of a nation.

In the next room, there were two doctors working together. When I came in, they immediately asked for my medical card (booklet the size of a local phone book that contains your medical history and records from your birth) or my military service record. I had neither. The one lady said I should come back when I did have one of them. I tried to explain that I NEVER had them and not just that I didn't have them *that* day. I pulled out our old, expired Russian medical examination sheet that we had to get in Russia three years prior when we adopted Jhenya *(which I happened to grab just in case I might need a distraction for my smoke and mirrors.)* I tried to explain that we had done something like this before. *(We had a Russian medical examination performed previously as our translated American version had expired since our adoption had been delayed. So that was eight doctor visits and about 24 official verification stamps and another long story ago.)* But this current tactic seemed to be working or at least threw them back a little bit.

The one doctor then asked what do we did if we got sick. I answered her by saying, "that we try not to and that we either treat ourselves or turn to one of our friends for help." She looked at me with a very quizzical smirk and decided to go ahead and process me. Because I was so nervous the only thing I remember them checking there was my blood pressure, which for some amazing reason turned out to be normal considering the circumstances. There was one other room, which I also blocked out, but whether from trauma, the rush through, or its insignificance, I can't remember.

The last room was something to do with coordination and reflexes. Who knows, it may have been something to do with neurology. When I went in, this doctor told me to take my shoes off and put them to the side. This I did well. Then she told me to sit down. I looked around. There was no

113

chair within a reasonable distance. I gave her one of those questioning glances as if displaying both my lack of understanding and my desire/request for more information. She repeated her direction to sit, and I still didn't get it. I finally spoke up and asked, "On the floor???" She gave me that look, said a few more words under her breath, and then caught on that I wasn't from around here. Then, she asked in a very choppy way, "Do you speak English?" (Must have been my Illinois/Ohio accent giving me away.) I said yes both in English and Russian, very loudly and slowly. She was wonderfully tickled. It turned out that her father had a love for learning English and had spread that to his five children. (That was a lot, even for way back then in Russia). So she repeated her direction, this time in English. "Sit down please." I answered, again in both languages, "where?" and "how?" Finally, she said in English, "Do as I," and she got up from her desk and began to squat, doing deep knee bends and holding out her hands. This I could do. I started to laugh and think to myself, "Well, why didn't she just say do deep knee bends, squat and hold the position with my arms out?" I passed that final station, and I was out the door back into the corridor, and the time was just under an hour.

We went back to the head doctor/registry to stand in line to pay and get the final stamps on the certificate, only to be told, however, that we still needed to get two more approvals. One from the "narcological" or drug center and the other from the psychiatrist . . . however, not in this building, somewhat clear across town, and since this was Friday, and she wanted to leave early, we had to be back in 45 minutes. Andrei and I looked at each other and decided, "what the . . .

114

what do we have to . . ., lets go." Worst scenario is we don't make it back in time, and I'll have to wait till next week to go through the joys of the technical inspection. "Ooh, somebody hold me down." And "where did I place those hot pokers?"

We hopped in the car and drove first to the drug center. Arriving there, we ran up the stairs, and Andrei held the certificate out in front of him like a baton in a relay race. The doctor looks up and informs us that we have to go to another building and pay 70 rubles (or about $2.50 give or take), and then come back with the receipt. Andrei tried the "Hey, he is an American" and began a short excursion into good political relations, etc. It didn't work, though it did get them to smile. We decided to run, instead of drive, the half block to the other building and find the cashier's office. We got to the cashier's window, and there was no one behind it. My luck. So, we waited impatiently looking around, and Andrei started to expand his search pattern. The only thing missing was the elevator music. Fortunately, she wasn't that long in returning. We paid and were off running back to get our stamp.

The women doctors there did not look up any records or even examine me. Just took that receipt, stamped my certificate, and we were off and running. I guess I just had one of those convincing "I am not addicted to anything" looks on. In this case, perhaps being an American living in northern Russia actually did help a little.

Not that there aren't more Americans addicted to something, and why not? We can afford it, and we have more free time than we know what to do with. Though, from her perspective, why would an American be this far north, in this particular city, running around for this certificate, if he was an addict of some sort? He may be crazy, but that's a matter for the psychiatrist. Not for the drug center. I got my stamp.

We jumped in the car and raced off to the psychiatrist. Once there, you have to check in with the registry office with your passport, get a little piece of paper that has a room number on it, and their sending/approval of you on it. This, to everyone's surprise, I got quickly.
We then rounded the corner to the door of the psychiatrist, and there was only one guy standing in line. Good news. This poor guy didn't know what hit him. Andrei, in front of me, immediately starts talking and mentioning the American thing and this or that, and the next thing I know as a girl exits the room, I am being ushered into it by Andrei. As he closed the door behind me, I can hear him continue to talk to the guy, probably in order to keep him distracted and not fully comprehending what just happened. I felt only slightly guilty and did my best to push the guilt aside and deal with it later. *Hey, I was in.*

This visit, though, looked like it was going to be a more serious visit. More than just paying for a stamp. The woman psychiatrist had that look about her. I don't know what or how, but it is often described as a slight chill that one feels upon approach. She looked at my documents and began to ask me a few questions as to what I was doing here. It actually went through my head to answer with the rhetorical question "would any sane American be sitting in this chair now?" I found myself thinking about the novel Catch 22 in reverse. (Something to the effect that to get out of the army you have to be crazy. But anyone who really wants out is

116

actually very sane given the reality of it. So you are caught.)
"So you're an American and you want to live and work in
Russia." *(Why does that always sound so suspicious?)* So,
how can I convince this woman that I am sane? (No help
from the peanut gallery, thank you.) That I want to be in
Russia and actually like it? *(Well, most of the time anyway.)*
This, too, when many Russians who can leave are doing it???
Oh, just shoot me now.

As it turned out, when I answered the question about
what I do and its connection with teaching the Bible, this
apparently hit on something of a personal interest with her.
Evidently, she has a good friend who is being led astray with
one of the many religious cults, and she wondered what my
affiliation was, if any, and what my opinion was about them.
I explained that we had no affiliation and went on to clarify
and define more clearly who we were, who invited us, and
what we are about doing. This seemed to interest her greatly.
I thought to myself, "Oh God, you are up to it again. I had
almost decided on doing a pragmatic end-around with all of
these documents and things and here you are putting me in a
conversation again with someone about you. The last time
You did this, I was more than half naked lying on an
examination table!
And, of course, we are pressed for time. Why now? Why
couldn't I get the certificate, and then have the 'divine
appointment' or conversation?"

We went on to talk about faith and her views about it,
and about how God seems to be more into the person rather
than the set ritual. I tried to encapsulate for her (given our
shortness on time) the heart of Christianity into a relationship
with God, established not on our self-deeds but on our

receiving of forgiveness through Jesus Christ, and as a resulting benefit, eternal life. There, of course, was a lot I left out, but the central gist was there, just not all the benefits or disclaimers.

Disclaimers, you might ask? Just those little ones like, if you really want to experience God and all those freedoms and changes in your life, then you might want to actually try *listening* to Him once in a while. And don't blame Him if you touched it and got burned or in trouble, He told you not to . . . or He told you how to handle it properly . . . . We just might have the tendency to want it the other way around. We want God to listen to US and make right and bless whatever we have in our plans, ideas, and activities. *(I sometimes imagine God with His head in His hands, shaking it from side to side saying, "Macarus, what will you think of next?" and "What am I going to do with you?" and "Oh, go on, and just don't get into any more trouble.")* "Oh and uhh God . . . just in case you are listening right now or reading this, I'm just kidding . . . ."

In the present time, I kept glancing at my watch and feeling the pressure that this was putting on that poor guy out in the hall, in a press for time to complete his certificate. On top of that, I got the distinct impression that this was taking much longer than the usual exam time.

After a bit more discussion, I politely informed her of my friend who was waiting out there for me who was helping me go through all of this. I asked for her name and thanked her for her time. I paid her directly *(a convenience she welcomed, though probably not completely kosher, if you know what I mean)*, and I was out the door, and we were on our way back to clinic. We made it just in time . . . .

Well, that part was over. An incredible feeling of lightness would have probably been more lasting if it had not been the fact that all of *that* was only to get me to the point of *being able* to now go through *the technical inspection.* On par only with other such joys as having your tooth pulled, being poked with a soft cushion, or having to face The Spanish Inquisition.

So where does that leave us?

Oh yes, back at what started this whole thing: the inspection.

I'll try to make this brief . . . as if that were possible. I am also not sure whether to actually print this as it may affect my life here and my future inspection possibilities . . . . So I have this hypothetical friend . . . . who just received his medical certificate, *and* plans with his friend to try to pass the technical inspection of his car . . . . And for ease, I will use the first person references of "I" and "Andrei" as the friend of this hypothetical friend.

Saturday: agreed time to meet friend and go through inspection was 4 p.m. Actual departure time was about 6:30 p.m. due to inadvertent delays of returning coworker from "going fishing."

An important cultural note: in Russia they have two phrases that delineate the two different and very distinct main goals in fishing. The first "going fishing" has not so much the fish in mind as the time spent away from the wife, with the boys, and with more than one bottle. If they are actually going after some sustenance to bring back to the table, they would say, "going after fish" –definitely a more serious business. You can imagine what phrase gets used more, and the question upon "going fishing" of "when are we going to fish?" rarely surfaces.

The reason this is so important is that the inspection place closes on Saturdays at 7 p.m. So you can imagine again, just a little bit of the added stress, wondering what kind of lines, etc., we might find when we get there.

Saturday, 6:47 p.m. No line at the place. Good sign.

Saturday, 6:48 p.m. Doors appear locked. No movement —bad sign.

Andrei heads for the office door and, fortunately for us, he still has his security guard uniform on. Because of that, they open the doors to admit our car. *(Apparently, they got the impression the car was used for security purposes. And we didn't think it was that important of an issue to clarify.)*

Andrei again deals with the paper work, while I drive the car up to the middle station. *(I am pleasantly surprised that they had me bypass the first station where they test the brakes. Part of which is that after the previous visit to the mechanics, my brakes were not working very well, and they were making this rhythmic vibration and bumping effect. Fortunately for me, only when I was trying to stop. I had also applied a small amount of black electrical tape inconspicuously and fortuitously over the "check engine light".)* They still enter my vehicle information into the computer for the test and their records system.

At the second station, they test for all of the lights: brakes, turn signals, headlights and high beams. I was still behind the wheel, and so when it was the time to turn the high beams on, I held the switch down. I began to get nervous because just at that time, the second inspector comes up from behind and stands just to my left (my window is open and he is looking in). So, he sees me go through this motion. Admittedly, too, I don't notice much difference in my high beams versus my low beams. Soooo, my next move is to cycle through high and low beams and to look out the window and ask if they came on in an unsuspecting tone.

They wave me through to the next station where they look under the car, shake the suspension and the tires. This is usually when they tell me to get new ball joints. Andrei is still out there talking with the people.

Finally they wave me through, and I am waiting outside the garage for Andrei to exit with or without my new inspection card. He comes out about ten minutes later. Unfortunately, my car did not pass because of only one problem—the headlights needed adjusting. Now, where I come from, adjusting the headlights only means putting a screwdriver in the right place and lowering or raising the focus of the beam. This, I thought would only merit a stern warning and wagging of the finger, not a refusal. I was surprised by this and disappointed, but Andrei seemed to assure me that everything would work out in the end.

Now, I realize that on the surface there is nothing remarkable or perhaps humorous about the details of the inspection. It has been provided so that the reader may understand the historical background and better appreciate what was to be revealed next . . . *Act 2, Scene 1.*

First: upon self-inspection of headlights, it was revealed that I had a blown fuse and that neither the low nor the high beams were working. The only light that was coming on during the technical inspection was a small running light located in the side of the headlight housing.
Interesting or puzzling that the inspectors did not mention this. Must be a very bright running light. I replaced the fuse.

Then, I went to an auto-electrical person, and we fixed the problem with having to hold down the high beam switch, and the reason why the fuse blew in the first place.

Second: Andrei finds out from his friend who works at the inspection facility that the facility wasn't even in working order and was essentially closed; hence, the reason for "no line" when we pulled up and why my brakes passed. It also created a slight problem in figuring out how to go back through an inspection line that wasn't working in the first place.

Third: Andrei also finds out later that the inspectors themselves offer to "adjust headlights" for a small fee and perhaps, more likely than not, that is what they were hoping or waiting for; hence, the first refusal.

Fourth: After reviewing all of our options, we decided to *thank* ahead of time this acquaintance of Andrei's who helped us to right the problem in the computer. In truth, it was not really the case that they were correcting something like a spelling error, such as "need adjustment" changed to "fixed/repaired, good working order." It was more expediting the process of affirming what was already now true—fuse replaced and headlights in working order and adjusted so that they actually come on when needed. (Though still, no change in placement of electrical tape.) So, out of consideration for the busy workday of the inspectors, it was felt this would save some time for all involved. So to keep things fair, we also passed on our thanks to the inspectors themselves for all of their help.

Just to set things straight, we do not pay bribes. We do however, like to thank those who help us out from time to time as the situation calls for. And it just so happens that sometimes the gifts of thankfulness can coincide very closely on either side of the received action: sometimes before and sometimes after. And after awhile, here, the distinction doesn't seem to matter so much anymore.

It is either this or I will be buying those adult diapers that everyone is talking about, as I will be so tickled when I actually accomplish something on the first try or that no one yells at me for one day in a row.

Just in case you were wondering, a typical gift for many is a box of chocolates, a bottle of wine, or a bottle of vodka, or any combination of the aforementioned. Russia runs on relationships. They have an old saying that it is better to have 100 friends than 100 rubles. (It must be old as 100 rubles is only about 3 dollars today. A more up-to-date translation: *it is better to have 100 friends than 1000 dollars.*) It would be nearly impossible to survive here without having some friends in the right places.

So there you have the irony and the reasons for writing this letter. I hope it helps, just a little, to brighten your day knowing how the other half lives.

———————

Postscript: the following occurred several months later.

We decided that we would like to buy a new Russian car to be able to use and drive to Finland in order to renew our visas. Whether this is wise or not is way beyond us at this point. Our ability to think rationally grossly affected, especially when you consider the previous letter written about "Selling a Car in Russia."

To cut to the chase: problem/challenge number 1. For us to drive to Finland, the car has to be in our own name, or for a Russian to own it and go with us, or for a Russian who has notarized permission to drive the car to cross over together.

Problem/challenge number 2: a foreigner can only register his car in his own name only for the length of his visa. Hence, every year we will have to renew our registration; hence, a few more lines and a little more money.

Problem/challenge number 3: if our registration ends with our visa, how can we drive to Finland to renew our visas on a car whose registration expires when we will be out of the country? How will we get back in?

Problem/challenge number 4: the car we just purchased is four-wheel drive. This means by Russian law, we have to register it, too, with the Military Command. Just in case there is a war, they can take the car to use for military purposes. Now how does that sound, an American supporting the war effort in Russia by "*donating* his car"? Why would anyone want to run the risk or take the chance? Why bother with a four-wheel drive vehicle? Especially when we only live this far north and have only eight months of winter? As my one friend and fellow teammate says, "it's all a crapshoot anyway."

So what do we do? Solution: overlap a little.

1. We buy a new car, register it in our own name, for a whole term of two weeks, since our visas expire on the 6th of September.

2. Get our friend to help us get it registered in both places, and in every way possible.

3. Plan to renew our visas and be back before the old registration expires.

4. Pray for no delays or difficulties on the way there or back.

5. Realize, too late, that I don't have any blank pages in my passport for the Russians to apply the visa to. Write to the US embassy in Helsinki at 5 a.m. and ask them for an appointment while we are there to add pages.

6. Get stressed out about the timing of everything and the unknown length of lines, etc., and wonder if this will put us off in timing and coming back nearer to the end of our old visas and our registration of the car. *It never seems to end.*

7. Pray and hit the gas . . . .

Addendum: interesting irony—in order to register the car, we needed that medical certificate that we had obtained by running around a few months ago. Good thing we didn't bypass that in a pragmatic way.

Secondly, to buy a new car, you have to go through the Technical Inspection station twice. Once where they just check the numbers on the engine and frame against the documentation. This registers the car to you in the computer for road taxes. The second time is when you get the inspection of the workings of the car. If you're clever and you know what you are doing, and or know someone, it may be possible to do these together at the same time.

By another interesting irony, we went through the same lines as above that we did with our old car. This time they checked the brakes but nothing else. Got the results, and it turned out that I had the same negative response show up on the computer print out about the headlights. *"Not working correctly."* I asked Andrei about it, saying, "They didn't even check the headlights!?!" This time though, apparently I passed since it was a new car and they figured they didn't need to check anything else.

Sometimes the "primordial scream" just isn't enough.

Jonathan Macarus is currently a Principal Research Engineer with METSS Corporation. He earned his Bachelor of Science degree in Chemical Engineering from The Ohio State University. He has over twenty years of professional experience. Ten of those years spent as a Research Scientist in polymer product and process development at Battelle Memorial Institute; and ten years spent as a Field and Team Leader living and working in Northwest Russia. It was during the last ten years in Russia that Jonathan had a chance to reflect on a few misadventures, life and all of its oddities, and to put some of them down in writing.

Made in the USA